The Cost of Free Speech

SIMON LEE

faber and faber
LONDON · BOSTON

First published in 1990
by Faber and Faber Limited
3 Queen Square London WC1N 3AU

Photoset by Parker Typesetting Service Leicester
Printed in Great Britain by
Cox and Wyman Ltd Reading Berkshire

A CIP record for this book is available from the British Library

ISBN 0-571-14447-0

With love and thanks to Patricia, Jamie, Katie and Rebecca, and to all those whose sacrifices for free speech help us to flourish.

Contents

Preface

Part I INTRODUCTION
1 Voltaire's Omelette 3
2 The Privatization of Censorship 10
3 The Costs of Free Speech 20

Part II VALUES
4 Privacy 29
5 Pornography 35
6 Incitement to Racial Hatred 39
7 Flag-Waving 44
8 Official Secrets 48

Part III ARGUMENTS
9 Slippery Slippery Slopes 55
10 What Is Speech? 59
11 Justifications 61

Part IV SALMAN RUSHDIE AND THE SATANIC VERSES
12 The Story 73
13 Blasphemy and the Law 76
14 Beyond the Law 94
15 'In Good Faith' 98
16 In Context 103

Part V SINN FEIN
17 Terrorists on Television 109
18 Under the Law? 115

Part VI CONCLUSIONS
19 Glasnost 125
20 Toleration 130
21 Reflections 132

Notes and Acknowledgements 141
Index 145

Preface

Speech is not free. It costs lives; or its price can be another value we hold dear. I believe that the cost of free speech is usually a price worth paying. Yet so many of those who purport to value free speech betray their ideals by failing to analyse exactly why freedom of expression is important, or from whom threats to free speech arise, or when it is wrong to exercise the right to free speech.

For example, in the sad Rushdie affair, the standard dogma of liberal folk has been an absolute commitment to freedom of expression for Rushdie and to dismiss as heresy any criticism of Rushdie. Those who wish to express themselves by burning his book are condemned as blasphemers against the sacred speech of the secular.

This book encourages readers to examine their own debating ploys in arguments over free speech. My belief is that free speech is under threat mostly from ourselves and, in particular, from our refusal to face up to the weaknesses in our own reasoning and to changes in the world. Television has become the dominant medium, censorship has been privatized, glasnost has broken out all over Eastern Europe, but we still argue as though we are back with the Founding Fathers of the United States of America over two centuries ago, worrying how to prevent the government from suppressing seditious pamphlets.

I am grateful to Faber and Faber in general and Will Sulkin in particular for publishing a book which challenges the kinds of arguments publishers use in defence of free speech. Their willingness to do so is itself an eloquent testimony to the fact that they have absorbed the lessons of this book.

A book which defends free speech against both its friends and its enemies ought to be dedicated to those who have given their lives for freedom of expression. You have probably never heard the names of the Belgian Muslim leader Imam Abdullah Al-Ahdal and his aide Salem el-Behir. They were assassinated for speaking out against the death-threat to Rushdie. Closer to home you may have forgotten the name of Edgar Graham, a law lecturer at Queen's University, Belfast, who was murdered by the IRA for being the articulate voice of a new generation of Unionists, or of Pat Finucane, a Belfast lawyer killed by 'Loyalist' terrorists after a government minister had indicated that some solicitors were in sympathy with the IRA. In a sense, then, this book is dedicated to all the Abdullah Al-Ahdals, Edgar Grahams and Pat Finucanes of this world.

But my personal dedication is to Patricia, my wife, and Jamie, Katie and Rebecca, our children. They paid the relatively small price for free speech of losing me to my study from time to time. Nevertheless in another sense they were a great influence, as well as a great support. For it has never been far from my mind that our young children are enjoying the wonderful world of words as they devour books while only a mile or so away other children are left fatherless as the men of violence devour those who dare to voice their views of law or justice. 'I have the audacity to believe' that clear thinking on free speech can contribute to the kind of world Martin Luther King envisaged in accepting his Nobel Peace Prize, a world in which 'none shall be afraid' and to which we will return in the final chapter.

Part I INTRODUCTION

We are all familiar with Voltaire's dramatic declaration in support of free speech: 'I disapprove of what you say but I will defend to the death your right to say it.' But, disappointingly, Voltaire said no such thing. His comment was, in fact, 'What a fuss over an omelette'. Since this hardly amounts to a ringing or eloquent endorsement of free speech, it is not surprising that we prefer to quote the line invented later by Evelyn Beatrice Hall as a summary of Voltaire's attitude.

But even if it were authentic, the sentence is far from convincing. Nowadays, it is endlessly invoked in such contexts as the travails of Salman Rushdie. This is indeed the proper setting since Voltaire was supposed to have said these words in reaction to the rough treatment accorded a fellow author and philosopher whose book was publicly burnt by the hangman. The philosopher was Claude Adrien Helvetius, whose 1758 book *De l'Esprit* was condemned by the Pope and the Parlement of Paris, withdrawn from publication and burnt. Shades of Rushdie, or, rather, Rushdie's troubles echo those of Helvetius. Helvetius held what might now be regarded as fashionable views, his book amounting to a critique of the notions of virtues and vices and an explication of an alternative idea that selfishness and emotions are the impulses which animate human beings. Like Rushdie, he disclaimed all responsibility for the furore which followed publication. Like Rushdie, he offered an apology. Unlike Rushdie, his apology was accepted and he was able to return to normal life after a two-year exile.

My worry in all this is that it has become too easy to invoke Voltaire in support of Rushdie without actually meaning any part of the apocryphal utterance. Do people who defend Rushdie really disapprove of what he has said? Do they really intend to defend him to the point of death? Are they really relying solely on his right to say it? This is but one example of a general malaise afflicting our support of free speech. We have allowed ourselves to rest on meaningless phrases, to dodge the difficult questions. We should instead accept that Voltaire is dead and worry about where this leaves free speech. It is time to develop new arguments to apply to new forms of speech in a new world, but first we must rid ourselves of the comforting clichés about defending to the death or sliding down slippery slopes.

We know that there are plenty of people who disapprove of what Rushdie has written and who will *attack* to the death his right to say it. But why on earth should anyone else rush to die for Rushdie, especially those who disapprove of what he has written? For all the huffing and puffing of the literary jet-set, the only 'Voltaire' to have emerged from the Rushdie saga has been the Belgian Muslim leader who was assassinated for opposing the Ayatollah's *fatwa*. He is the only person, at the time of writing, who fits the category of disapproving of what Rushdie said but defending to his own death Rushdie's right to say it. For the rest of us, it is easy to cast ourselves as Voltaires but we should ask ourselves whether we are entitled to say any more than 'I approve of what Salman Rushdie wrote and I will defend his right to say it unto the last letters column of the last quality newspaper or unto the most dangerous TV chat-show.'

In fact, the most plausible reaction for many of us to the Ayatollah's response might best be summarized, in Voltaire's less well remembered phrase, as 'What a fuss over an omelette.' For it is difficult for many of us to understand why other people are outraged by *The Satanic Verses*. Those who have no sense of the sacred, for example, are liable to think that Muslims are making a fuss over nothing. A simple test for would-be Voltaires is to ask about their attitude to the Bradford book-burnings. Would they defend the right of outraged Muslims to burn their copies of Rushdie's book – given that there is nothing unlawful in so doing and given that it is a dramatic way of expressing disgust?

As it happens, the very people who have been echoing Voltaire in defence of Rushdie were the first to denounce the Bradford Muslims' freedom of expression. No wonder, then, that Muslims might think that the Voltaire line is pure humbug in the mouths of many. In their eyes, it must seem that there is one rule for those who make a living out of offending religious sensibilities by insulting the Prophet but another for those who offend the feelings of the secular literary set, for whom only books are apparently sacred. If Rushdie is free to express his view that Islam is intolerant, Muslims should be free to express their view that the book is only fit to be burnt. Personally, I find it difficult to work myself up into a frenzy of indignation over the burning of the American flag or the burning of a book, even though I am well aware of the Nazi precedents. Nor can I find it within me to get annoyed by blasphemous books. However, I quite accept that others do find one or more of these activities outrageous.

Many commentators, then, are selective in their outrage and slack in their application of the Voltaire dictum. The test of their commitment to freedom of expression should come when they encounter something of which they disapprove, such as book-burning. This is the very moment at which they are oblivious to the irony of their discriminatory indignation.

Turning away from the Rushdie saga, I have not noticed many commentators who are willing to die for the free speech of those who live in Belfast. Even if they were so willing, they would probably be dying for the wrong people anyway. They are prepared to make a fuss over Sinn Fein's free speech when it is under threat from the government but not to stand up against Sinn Fein and the IRA for the free speech of those who are too frightened of reprisals from the men of violence to speak out in their own community. In O'Casey's memorable words, echoed by Catholic bishops and priests at many funerals in Northern Ireland, it is not the IRA who are dying for the Irish people but the Irish people who are dying for the IRA. For all the fuss over the threat to Rushdie from Iranian terrorists, and for all the fuss over the relatively minor threat to Irish terrorists from the denial of the oxygen of publicity, there seems little invocation of the Voltaire sentiment when it might actually have to be put into practice in Belfast. I am the first to admit to failure in this respect. I disapprove of what many loyalist and republican politicians are saying and I am only too well aware that they are under constant threat of assassination from one or other side but the coward in me would rather enjoy life with my family than die for their right to free speech.

More generally, what do we mean by invoking Voltaire? Are we genuinely prepared to become martyrs for speech of which we *dis*approve? Would we really defend it to the *death*? Or perhaps the nearest we are going to get to support for free speech is to bemoan the fuss over an omelette. Of course, when pressed, we might say that it is a piece of rhetoric that is not meant to be taken literally. The point is rather that we would be prepared to make a fuss on behalf of somebody who was being censored, whether or not we agreed with the thrust of their comments. Voltaire's attributed words may be hyperbolic but they do convey the depth of commitment we feel to free speech, even if we do not match our strong words with appropriate action.

Let us, for a moment, consider the quotation at this level. What remains problematic is our commitment to speech of which we *disap-prove*, as indicated by the preamble, which is picked up at the end of the sentence. 'I disapprove of what you say' is reinforced at the end by the emphasis on the '*right*' (that is, regardless of whether I think you are wise to exercise the right). As it happens, some people *have* defended Rushdie because of his right, even though they take strong exception to what he has said. Mrs Thatcher, 'Mrs Torture' in *The Satanic Verses* and Sir Geoffrey Howe spring to mind. They were severely criticized by friends of Rushdie for making it clear that they disapproved of the book.

If it is somehow unacceptable to say that one does not like the book, it suggests that many of the most vociferous supporters of Rushdie are in the position of approving of the book, in which case Voltaire does not come into play. This is, I suspect, the standard response. I would be much happier to stand up, maybe not to death but at least to Terry Wogan, for speech of which I approve – that is to say when I felt that someone else was right to say it. When I hear the phrase that they had *a* right to say it, I am more wary. This is not because I misunderstand the nature of a right (much of my professional life is taken up with rights-talk) but I am increasingly frustrated by the two-dimensional way in which much moral discourse is conducted, as if we either believe in utilitarianism or in rights. Sometimes a third option is offered which seeks to reconcile utilitarianism and rights. My own view, however, is that our moral frameworks can legitimately reflect a range of values, only some of which can be properly described as rights, and that we can usefully comment on the rightness and wrongness of exercising rights without collapsing into utilitarian calculus.

Let me explain with a simple example. Do you believe in free speech? Yes. Do you believe in Father Christmas? No. Do you have the legal right to tell a young child that Father Christmas does not exist? Yes. Would you be morally right to do so? No.

Nobody wants a world in which the law stoops to ban free expression of the truth about Father Christmas but many of us hope that other adults will voluntarily restrain their speech so as to allow our children to enjoy the Father Christmas story. Suppose a Scrooge went around your neighbourhood telling toddlers that Father Christmas did not exist. If you took umbrage, he might defend himself by saying, 'It's a free country, isn't it? I'm free to say what I like, especially when it's true.' You would have to agree, although you would probably add a 'but', indicating that he has missed the point of living in society. He has the right of free speech but he was wrong to exercise the right in this way. To be perfectly honest, I would not defend to the death the right of some such Scrooge to exercise his right to free speech. I am, to be blunt, not so much interested in his legal or moral rights as in the different question of whether he was right or wrong to speak in that way.

Yet we so often shy away from judging the rights and wrongs of exercising rights. Indeed, part of the point of rights-talk is to avoid such judgement or at least to defend those who are making unpopular use of their rights. Nobody wants to ban the soggy centre of British politics because they never say anything which could annoy anybody. When the bland are leading the bland, nobody is sufficiently outraged to want to restrain free speech. So the right to free speech is most useful precisely when it is being exercised 'wrongly' or in an unpopular manner. Hence the National Front or the Ku Klux Klan or Sinn Fein are the kind of groups who will benefit from focusing on the right rather than the merits of exercising the right. If they deserve this benefit, of course, then this is not a reason against concentration on the rights. Their freedom would simply be one of the costs of free speech, which are the subject of this book.

But do we really feel that we can never say anything about the morality of exercising a right? Moving from Father Christmas to another example which led to worldwide litigation, many commentators (and quite a few judges) have said that Peter Wright was wrong to publish *Spycatcher* but that he had the legal right to do so, at least outside the United Kingdom. On a smaller scale, most of us possess information which could be damaging to other individuals, and we are always balancing our right to pass on this information with other values, such as respecting privacy or avoiding distress to innocent third parties.

Such moral criticism itself rests on a presupposition which admits that it might sometimes be wrong to exercise the right to free speech. Just because the law, for good reasons, does not go further than to ask about the rights, this does not mean that we should stop arguing about the merits of exercising the right to free speech.

Thus there is nothing wrong or pusillanimous in asking whether Rushdie might wish to forego his right to have the paperback edition of *The Satanic Verses* published (although I should stress that I am not suggesting Rushdie should answer this question one way or the other). The book has already sold a million copies in hardback in the UK and the USA. It has been translated into many languages and has been published around the globe. Rushdie does not have a duty to publish, he has a right, but the mere acknowledgement of the right does not compel action. He has to make a further moral decision as to whether he feels it is proper to exercise the right.

This kind of decision will, increasingly, be the crucial point in free speech debates. It is the type of decision we all take all the time. Yet undue reliance on Voltaire's alleged remark has led some people to believe that it constitutes forbidden territory. We take decisions by default, without careful analysis, in the mistaken belief that the arguments are all to do with law and rights. It is time to pursue the arguments into the land and language of right and wrong.

Move over, Voltaire. Even if someone has the right to say something, so what? What is most important nowadays is the answer to a different kind of question, increasingly asked in publishing or on television or in the press: 'I disapprove of what you say, I know that you have got the legal right to say it, but tell me, why should I put up the money for you (or put my job on the line for you) to make a sick joke/rude comment/ crude insult?' Or even a 'great joke/perceptive comment/sophisticated critique?'

Thus, every part of Voltaire's most famous non-saying leads us astray. I have heard the phrase used so many times by people who *approve* of what has been said, who have no intention of *dying* for free speech, and who seem to have no inkling of the fact that there is more to free speech than the legal *right*, that I am tempted to say that it has passed into George Orwell's Newspeak. You will recall that in *1984*, the Ministry of Truth's building carried the three slogans of the Party:

WAR IS PEACE
FREEDOM IS SLAVERY
IGNORANCE IS STRENGTH

In the calendar year of 1984, as in the book, this type of Newspeak was in operation all over the world. The fall of the Romanian dictator, Ceausescu, for example, led to revelations about his deliberate manipulation of 'news'. The rise of the Czech and Slovak peoples can be seen in part as the effort to claw back the true meaning of words like 'peace' – to take one example cited by Vaclav Havel – from their misuse by oppressive governments.

Of course we have the right to speak freely and to rely on the comfort afforded by Voltaire. But I am suggesting that the time has come to be more self-critical, to stop fooling ourselves that we are willing to die for speech of which we disapprove and to look for better arguments. If his remark 'What a fuss over an omelette' had been repeated accurately through the ages we would be less likely to invest it with moral authority and more willing to look for more rigorous arguments.

What I suspect we take the invented Voltaire sentence to mean is something much less grand than its wording suggests, more on the lines of if I approve of what you say, if it does not cost me too much in terms of time or money or danger, and if you can convince me that you were right to exercise your right to free speech, then I will defend you. If all those conditions are met, there is unlikely to be a fuss in the first place: you would have produced an omelette rather than something to set the world alight. So why should we go further and defend those whose speech we find distasteful? And against whom should we set up our defence?

2   The Privatization of Censorship

If we agree to jettison the Voltaire declaration, we're in need of some other, more realistic, support for free speech. And if we must have a catchphrase to encapsulate our attitude to that freedom, I would prefer to rely on the wise words of an Irish lawyer and politician, John Philpot Curran. Two hundred years ago, on 10 July 1790, on the occasion of the election of the Lord Mayor of Dublin, he declared that 'The condition upon which God hath given liberty to man is eternal vigilance; which condition if he breaks, servitude is at once the consequence of his crime and the punishment of his fault.' Curran is actually a formidable figure in Irish history but outside Ireland he is probably best remembered, if he is remembered at all, for this (accurate) quotation. Even those who dispute the divine identity of the donor would probably agree with the general thrust of what Curran says about the need for vigilance.

But it is little use being vigilant if we have no idea of the likely direction of assault. Hence free speech has been continuously clobbered by all sorts of private attackers who steal in by the back door while the liberal elite keep guard against the government at the front gate. Threats to free speech come from all directions, not just from government. To this extent, censorship has been privatized, taken out of the hands of the state and located in other sources of power.

To ignore this is to betray a remarkable lack of historical perspective. The high priests of liberalism were only too well aware of the threats to liberty from non-governmental sources. John Stuart Mill (1806–73), for example, warned of the dangers posed by the tyranny of public opinion, which he saw as far more coercive than the law because 'it leaves fewer means of escape, penetrating much more deeply into the details of life, and enslaving the soul itself'. It is complacency, rather than vigilance, to believe that the law and the government are mostly to blame for restrictions on free speech. *We* are to blame. It is time to recapture Mill's vigilance against all manner of threats to free speech. Of course, since Mill the manipulation of public opinion has become more sophisticated and the sources of private censorial power more diverse, hence greater vigilance is required.

In our everyday lives, censors are all around us. We censor one another through withering looks, subtle threats of sticks or promises of carrots. There is constant pressure to conform. 'Orthodoxy means not thinking – not needing to think' as Syme told Winston Smith in Orwell's *1984*. One of the major steps we could take towards free speech does not require anything as dramatic as death. Instead, we should simply be more open to debate in our private lives, so that we might build up the appropriate culture in which free speech can flourish.

If we turn to the mass media, however, as more likely to be involved in major threats to free speech, where should we look for such threats? First, there are the owners of the media, press barons like Rupert Murdoch, Robert Maxwell and Tiny Rowland. Second, the management. Third, the employees, as with the print unions in the old days of Fleet Street. Fourth, the advertisers. Fifth, the consumers. Sixth, those who use violence or threats of violence to intimidate, such as the Ayatollahs. Seventh, the self-regulatory bodies, such as the Press Council. Eighth, the statutory bodies, such as the Broadcasting Standards Council. This is not to deny that the ninth and tenth censors, the unelected and elected branches of government, are potentially more powerful constraints on the media, but it is to argue for a more rounded picture of the threats to press freedom and to suggest that more care should be taken over the direction of our vigilant watch. Censors come like thieves in the night. Unfortunately, the confusing reality is that the thieves are often at one and the same time the householders. Those who restrict the speech are often those who also make it possible. Hence we have to be on guard against ourselves, which is much less dramatic than having a government trample over our dead bodies on its way to silencing free speech, but it is the only realistic answer to the question 'quis ipsos custodes custodiet?' – 'who shall keep guard over the guards themselves?' Answer: 'the guards'. Curran was absolutely right to emphasize the need to be on our guard to protect our liberty. I hope I am right in suggesting that some of the following unlikely candidates have to be watched.

Owners

The first 'censors' or restricters of media freedom are the owners of the
media, from the newspaper barons to the directors of publishing houses.
And why not, you might say. Why should Rupert Murdoch pay for a
newspaper which works against his political views? One answer would
be that he does not so much 'pay' as 'make money' from his news empire.
A second would be the old-fashioned (i.e. pre-Thatcherite) view that
news, like water, is a public good. Neither answer is convincing, especially in
an era where profit is king and where water has been privatized.

It is only to be expected that proprietors will influence their papers, at the
very least in the choice of editor, though often more directly. What is more
disappointing is the refusal of so much of the media to admit this. Thus the
Observer's obsession with the business rivals of its owners, Lonrho, is
tedious and self-serving but also important and not surprising, though the
editor's denial of any proprietorial influence is thought by some to devalue
the currency of a once great liberal paper. The papers trade on a reputation
for impartiality (albeit illusory) that the quality press used to have.

Once we question the term 'news' paper and substitute 'entertainment'
paper, then the idea of the press as a business seems less galling, and we
can understand that control of the papers is a question of profits and
power, in the race for which the press will invoke its freedom from legal
restraints while doing its masters' bidding. It is no coincidence that the
modern press barons include some of the richest businessmen in the
country. (Robert Maxwell's desperate search for a newspaper he could
control eventually yielded the Mirror group, but at times during the
eighties his quarry seemed to be quite simply a newspaper, any newspaper.) One reason is the desire to exercise power. It helps to have a
mouthpiece for one's other business interests, as Murdoch's News
International group demonstrated by puffing up Sky satellite television in
the allegedly 'news' pages of *The Times*, the *Sun* and co. Another reason
is that the newspapers are themselves big businesses, the Mirror group's
prime site in Holborn, for example, being a major asset. As shrewd
capitalists, the press magnates realized that the new technology and
newly tamed unions presented an opportunity for increasing efficiency
and profits. It is unrealistic to expect these properties to support newspapers which work against their own interests. Equally, it is unrealistic
for their editors to deny proprietorial influence.

Management

Of course, the editors have minds of their own, but their vision can itself act as a constraint on the freedom of their journalists and particularly of their freelance contributors. It can be difficult to disentangle proprietors' wishes and editors' wishes in the running of newspapers and there have been plenty of examples of contributors departing in high dudgeon or otherwise complaining about editorial censorship.

However, the role of editors or management is easier to see in broadcasting. In particular, the reputation of John Birt as the *de facto* chief of broadcasting matters at the BBC (albeit as number two to the Director-General Michael Checkland) is of a man who has had no hesitation in imposing controls on his journalists and who is in that sense a 'censor' even though he has been quick to complain about the government's censorship (although slow to do anything more than complain, leaving legal action to others). Of course, Mr Birt might object that an editor must edit and if we call that censorship, then the editor is by definition a censor. Quite so. My point is not a semantic one but a political or power-related point which seeks to emphasize the multi-layered nature of restraints on the mythically 'free' journalist. This is not to criticize the people who are doing their jobs so much as to point out that jobs other than those of judge or Prime Minister have an inhibiting, as well as an enabling, function in relation to the media.

Other parts of the media are also subject to inevitable censorship by their management. Publishing houses are being taken over almost as frequently as the industry awards itself literary prizes. Speech costs money to put on paper, print and publish. The management will not invest in the anarchic but brilliant ideas of an unknown leftist academic, for example, when they can instead publish the memoirs of another Conservative ex-Cabinet Minister, however appalling their life and literary abilities. Publishers were falling over themselves to *avoid* publishing *The Rushdie File* by Appignanesi and Maitland in case it led to Voltaire's epigram being put to the test. Instead they put a few hundred pounds into the kitty of the committee to protect Salman Rushdie and wrote letters to the press complaining about the government's failure to support free speech. This is understandable, given concerns for the safety of their staff and given our admission that we are not setting ourselves Voltairean standards of self-sacrifice.

In a more humdrum way, however, there will always rightly be arguments about the role of commissioning editors. Is their guiding light profit or quality or conformity? If they do not like the suggested subject of a biography, is it censorship to turn down an otherwise convincing book proposal? Of course, publishers will argue that a free market enables most plausible authors to get most plausible books into print and that the decision by an individual company not to proceed is in no way an infringement of free speech. There would be no fun or skill left in the job if they were to publish everything submitted and next I would be complaining about the public refusing to buy (well, yes, I will come to that soon).

What about a slightly different case, however, where a book is accepted but the publishers want passages taken out for fear of libel? Or where they would rather a passage come out because, while not libellous, it might offend another one of their authors? Viking Penguin clearly did not take this line with Rushdie's novel even though they were simultaneously publishing Benazir Bhutto's autobiography, so that her government ended up banning her publishers. Next time round, the self-censorship question may loom larger, or there may be a temptation to avoid the issue by steering clear of so controversial a subject as Islam – which takes us back to the preceding paragraph.

In this way, the actions of one privatized censor, an international terrorist (will Faber allow this phrase as a description of the Ayatollah?), will inevitably cause problems for other privatized free speech promoters/censors. These problems aren't easy to resolve but they must be debated. It is clearly inadequate to stop at the point where government bans are the only cause for concern.

Employees

The influence of trade unions in Fleet Street, who printed, and from time to time refused to print, the newspapers was legendary. A combination of the government's restrictions on the unions, the entrepreneurship of Eddie Shah and Rupert Murdoch, and above all of the new technology, has allowed the press to by-pass this form of censorship during the Thatcher years. Nevertheless it was not so long ago that *The Times* closed down for a year over an industrial dispute or that the *Observer* was embroiled in controversy when its unions censored Bernard Levin's book reviews. Nowadays, other employees have more subtle forms of control over what we get to read. Suppose the National Union of Journalists, for example, were to adopt a policy which commits its members to do everything in their power to support the pro-choice side on the abortion question. Such a union would be interested not in free speech so much as speech which suits it. Would this explain why you are unlikely to read a pro-life article in most newspapers or magazines? I disapprove of what you want to say so I am not going to report it.

Advertisers

Another group of censors is the advertisers who make newspapers commercially viable. It was neither the law nor the government which brought the pornographic tendencies of the *Daily Star* and *Sunday Sport* under some kind of control but the power of Tesco and other major advertisers who did not wish to be associated with a paper which so shamelessly exploited women, who form the majority of their employees and customers. This is also a concern in the future world of satellite television. Already advertisers have dictated the content of independent terrestrial television so that the popular, if excruciating, soap opera *Crossroads* was stopped because advertisers wanted more targeted shows attracting high-spending potential customers. Although *Crossroads*' viewing figures were high, the spending capacity of its viewers was not, so it was axed. Again, you may argue that those who pay the piper should call the tune, and in the case of Tesco we might all applaud their 'censorship', but as we move towards sponsored programmes and greater commercial pressure on television, we need to be aware of the power placed in private hands, by this approach to the speech that reaches us.

Intimidation

Those who intimidate the media are among the most effective censors. I am not primarily referring to Northern Ireland, since the terrorists here agree with Mrs Thatcher on the importance of the media in providing the oxygen of publicity, but to another medium and a different environment – the book publishing world, which has seen the most dramatic threat of violence to the media. The Ayatollah Khomeini's death threat turned the publishing world upside down. There is no doubt that publishers ran scared – witness what happened to *The Rushdie File* – as lives were lost, employees were threatened, buildings were blown up, all in an effort to censor. The threats did extract an apology from Salman Rushdie, although it was deemed to be too grudging. It is quite certain that this experience will continue to affect the way in which the media deal with Islamic and other subjects.

Self-regulatory bodies

It is becoming increasingly difficult and unrealistic to distinguish the private bodies of censors from the public. Some such bodies are set up by the industries themselves, such as the Advertising Standards Authority and the Press Council, while others are imposed by the government, such as the Broadcasting Standards Council. In the absence of an effective example of the first sort, an industry is always likely to be landed with the second. For example, the Press Council had a bad press during the 1980s. It was widely derided as a toothless watchdog. Steps were taken towards the end of the decade to restructure it, most notably through the appointment of the high profile Louis Blom-Cooper QC. The press editors even took action to put their own houses in apparent order by complementary measures such as adopting a code of practice on privacy and appointing their own ombudsmen. All this was in an effort to forestall legislative intervention, anticipated in the wake of an announcement that the Home Office was to set up a committee to report on privacy and the press. None of the industry's self-regulatory measures seem to have stopped the trend towards greater intrusion by the press into private lives.

Statutory bodies

Would a statutory body fare any better? The government has so far created the Broadcasting Standards Council (BSC) under the leadership of Lord Rees-Mogg as a check on radio and, especially, television standards of 'decency'. Its response has been to promulgate a code of practice to add to all the other codes of practice now available to the media (see, for example, the BBC's exhaustive instructions, also published as the decade ended). The principal function of the BSC is to provide a solution to an ideological problem for Mrs Thatcher. As a free marketeer in economic matters she wanted to open up the broadcasting airwaves to competition. As a paternalistic opponent of the free market in moral matters, however, she recognizes the possibility that untrammelled competition might lead to a lowering of standards on such issues as the portrayal of sex and violence. Hence the government decided to auction TV franchises to more or less the highest bidder (with some quality safeguards) while leaving the BSC to police standards.

Serious doubts have been expressed about the accountability of censors like the Press Council and the BSC. The great and good move from post to post, from alleged poacher to alleged gamekeeper. Lord Rees-Mogg was the key actor in the BBC Board of Governors' decision to accede to the Home Secretary's request not to broadcast a *Real Lives* programme in 1985. When he moved from regulated to regulator as Chairman of the BSC in 1989, we could be forgiven for expecting little change. The government does not *need* restrictive legislation when it can place restrictive, like-minded individuals in key media positions through its powers of patronage.

Judges

The more traditional personification of the law, the judiciary, had its own opportunities to censor the media during the 1980s. Unlike the BSC, or managers or editors, the judges do not have the power of initiative, but when the government or citizens or the media came to the courts, the judges were portrayed as doing their best to inhibit the freedom of the press. Of course, this image comes *from* the press and is not entirely accurate, but it is true to say that injunctions prevented newspapers from publishing details of Peter Wright's *Spycatcher* allegations for some two years, that journalists such as Jeremy Warner fell foul of the courts when they refused to disclose confidences, that magistrates restricted reporting and that challenges to the Home Secretary's order restricting broadcast coverage of the supporters of violence in Northern Ireland were rebuffed by the judges in 1989.

Government

When we think of censorship, however, the government first springs to mind. The thrust of this chapter has been to emphasize the other constraints on the media but there is no doubt that some of the government's reputation in this regard is justified. It is, though, important to recognise that the government rarely has to resort to the heavy-handed method of the Home Secretary's 1988 order banning direct speech on television by supporters of terrorism. It can achieve its aims by appointing its supporters to key posts, such as the BBC Board of Governors. It can influence the BBC through the power of the purse, at least in the run-up to licence fee negotiations. Discreet phone calls, or for that matter public letters, have sometimes been enough to prevent the broadcasting of material which the government wanted kept off the screen (as witness the *Real Lives* dispute). It may be that the media too readily give in to this pressure and that the government too readily applies it, but its existence has to be appreciated before we can understand why the law is *not* invoked in various circumstances and does not need to be.

Only after we have recognized the great variety of threats to free speech should we turn to the judges and the government, who between them are responsible for the network of laws on national security, contempt of court, privacy, obscenity and so on. Of course, these are powerful constraints on the media but if we are to understand free speech we need to evaluate them in comparison with the other restrictions. We will never even begin this task if we take the traditional route of focusing on the government and the law first and last. For example, the big problem for the media in Northern Ireland might seem to be the ludicrous TV 'ban' on the supporters of violence, but the bigger problem for those of us who live in Northern Ireland is the self-censorship of the British media, who barely cover Northern Ireland anyway. More attention has been paid to reporting the ban than there has ever been to reporting Northern Ireland.

The difficulty with this call for vigilance is that the gamekeepers are also the poachers. We need to examine the power of the media, the Fourth Estate, not only as the conduit for so much free speech but also as the control valve which determines what speech will be let loose upon the public. In this context, it is important to acknowledge that we live in a rapidly changing world of media technology. We need not only to look in the right direction but also to accept that we are looking at different phenomena from those which existed when, say, the American Founding Fathers developed their ideas on free speech some two hundred years ago. Before we can assess the strengths and weaknesses of arguments for free speech, therefore, we need to accept that free speech today plays different roles, through different media, in a world of different values. We need to appreciate the power of free speech, the variety of free speech and the costs of free speech.

3 The Costs of Free Speech

Word power

Just before the peaceful revolution in Czechoslovakia swept Václav Havel reluctantly to power, he received the Peace Prize of the German Booksellers' Association. In his acceptance speech he reflected on 'the mysterious power of words in human history'. He reminded us that 'all important events in the real world – whether admirable or monstrous – are always spearheaded in the realm of words.'

Reflecting on the saga of *The Satanic Verses*, Havel observed that 'alongside Rushdie's words we have Khomeini's. Words that electrify society with their freedom and truthfulness are matched by words that mesmerize, deceive, inflame, madden, beguile, words that are harmful – lethal, even. The word as arrow.' He concluded that 'words are a mysterious, ambiguous, ambivalent phenomenon. They are capable of being rays of light in a realm of darkness . . . They are equally capable of being lethal arrows. Worst of all, at times they can be the one and the other. And even both at once!' Hence 'words are capable of betraying us – unless we are constantly circumspect about their use'. Havel emphasized that 'it always pays to be suspicious of words and to be wary of them' and declared that 'There can be no doubt that distrust of words is less harmful than unwarranted trust in them.'

Not for Havel, then, the simple slogan 'speech is good' which seems to be as far as many freer commentators can get in their consideration of free speech. At the same time as pressing for freedom, we must develop and exercise the critical faculties necessary for discernment. It was a crucial strength of the Czech and Slovak people that through the years of censorship, they 'developed a profound distrust of all generalizations, ideological platitudes, clichés, slogans, intellectual stereotypes and insidious appeals'.

Havel, of course, is intimately familiar with censorship and repression. He knows the power of speech to beguile. He also knows the cost of free speech. He does not seek to hide the dangers of speech, nor to gloss over the costs. Here surely is a lesson for those of us who have lived in less oppressive circumstances. Honesty about the power and cost of free speech is a necessary precursor to useful analysis.

So often useful debate is precluded by a failure to admit the power of words. Lenin is alleged to have asked: 'Why should freedom of speech and freedom of the press be allowed? Why should a government which is doing what it believes to be right allow itself to be criticized? It would not allow opposition by lethal weapons. Ideas are much more fatal things than guns.' If we substitute 'words' for 'ideas' in this apocryphal quotation we can see that it makes an important point about speech, one also made by Havel when he says that 'words can prove mightier than ten military divisions'. Lenin's solution to the threat posed by words was the one too often adopted by governments, namely to meet reasoned opposition by brute force. It is naïve of us to suppose that governments and other censors can be conned into accepting that free speech carries no risks for them. Of course it does. It is vital that we are alert to the power of speech. Too often there is a tendency to play down the significance of words, to argue that the government might as well allow speech because it does not matter. It does. Free speech can, and has, cost governments their existence and government ministers their lives.

Changes in the mass media

A recognition of the changes in the mass media is also vital to a modern debate about free speech. Whereas the media have changed dramatically over the last two centuries, the same old arguments over free speech seem to carry on regardless. A few examples will suffice to indicate the pace and extent of change during the last decade, let alone the last century or two. As far as British broadcasting was concerned, the 1980s saw such innovations as Channel 4, Sky satellite television, breakfast television, all-night television, mass audiences for such domestic and foreign soap operas as *Eastenders* and *Neighbours*, videos, government anti-Aids advertisements on the BBC, independent producers providing programmes for the BBC, and commercial radio.

So what? To take one small example, there is now intense lobbying of the producers of soap operas to take up causes and to resolve them in the way which competing pressure groups would prefer. The popular press in England feeds off the screen and private lives of the soap opera stars. For example, the introduction of a gay couple into *Eastenders* was greeted with the front page banner headline EASTBENDERS. I have suggested elsewhere that Michelle's double abortion dilemma in the same show may well have had more impact on abortion decisions than any number of laws, sermons, lessons. On the first occasion, she had the baby. On the second, she had an abortion. The pressure on producers and scriptwriters must have been intense. Even the Prime Minister has stooped to giving advice to soap opera characters, recommending that Ken Barlow of *Coronation Street* should leave his mistress and return to his wife and adopted daughter. Interest groups are no longer content with the theoretical freedom to launch their own channel (although rich fundamentalist groups may try that once satellite television develops, as they have with cable television in the USA) or to speak freely when spoken to by some vox pop interviewer like Robert Kilroy-Silk. They want air-time of their own and fair coverage of their views in the programmes so many millions watch – the soap operas. This is not a demand one would like to see being resolved legally but it is an issue television executives are having to address. Do we believe that even if we disapprove of what people say, we should give them a soap-box in our soap opera?

The medium of print journalism also saw fundamental changes during the 1980s: the end of 'Fleet Street' trade union power, the launches of such papers as the *Independent, Today* and the *Sunday Correspondent*, colour photographs in newspapers, £1½ million libel damages and the Home Office Committee on Privacy and the Press. Other media also changed significantly. For example, publishing became big business with huge advances, publicity, prizes and sales for some novelists and biographers. It became more truly international and this brought problems as well as profits, most notably with the publication of Peter Wright's *Spycatcher* and Salman Rushdie's *The Satanic Verses*. The advertising industry blossomed and spread its influence through the other media. For a while, at least, Saatchi and Saatchi ruled the world. They certainly seemed to invent Thatcherism. If the medium was not quite the message, the controllers of the media controlled the message. Or to raise a completely different set of problems, the developing industry of information technology opened up possibilities of mass surveillance, for example, through British Telecom's newly installed programmable digital systems. It now seems that speech can be freely intercepted.

These changes have many causes, such as the development of new technology (e.g. satellite television), economics (e.g. the concentration of ownership of the press), the international dimension (e.g. affecting the publicity, sales and reception of *Spycatcher* and *The Satanic Verses*) and ideology (the idea of opening up a certain percentage of broadcasting on the main networks to independent producers, although having its economic rationale, seems to have been floated primarily to enhance the Thatcherite discipline of competition).

All these changes have many consequences, such as the power to make and crush governments. The wave of largely peaceful revolutions in Eastern Europe as the 1980s ended was very much aided by television, particularly in so far as East Germans were able to witness life in West Germany through TV. The media in general, and television in particular, have therefore come under pressure from all governments. In systems without elections, the media can bring about democracy. Where there already are elections, they can be won and lost on television, not necessarily through debates but via news coverage. No wonder then that one senior British politician spoke for many in saying that there should be 'a new framework of public service control and operation over the constitutional monarchs who reside in the palatial Broadcasting House. Broadcasting is really too important to be left to the broadcasters.' That minister was not some member of Mrs Thatcher's government defending the Broadcasting Bill in 1990 but the Labour left-winger Tony Benn, speaking in 1968 when Postmaster-General. Politicians on all sides are becoming only too well aware of the power of the modern media. As the Conservative Party's Marketing Director, Christopher Lawson, observed in the context of the 1983 general election, 'It's the same as advertising a product: you just say something more and more frequently and people will eventually understand and say it themselves.' The campaigning techniques of Presidents Reagan and Bush classically exemplified this use of the media, as they reduced their comments to twenty-second sound bites for news coverage and orchestrated their diaries to provide photo opportunities. On this side of the Atlantic, the example was followed. Nobody any longer emulates

Gladstone stumping the country haranguing audiences for hours on end. Yet they argue about free speech as if we were back in Victorian times, or earlier. Discussion often proceeds as if we were back with the American Founding Fathers, communicating through pamphlets and local public meetings. We need to revise our arguments in the light of today's free speech, accepting the costs as well as the undoubted benefits of modern communications.

Costs

Perhaps the single most important reason for this book to be written and read can be summarized thus. Speech is not free. It is costly. Careless talk, as the saying goes, costs lives. Careless talk by a government minister about the sympathies of defence lawyers in Northern Ireland is credited in some circles with unwittingly inspiring the murder of a Belfast lawyer, Pat Finucane. Careless talk by adults or older children can ruin the story of Father Christmas for a young child. One of the most common arguments in defence of *The Satanic Verses* is that the right to free speech allows the writer's imagination to flourish; yet by *inhibiting* free speech we can preserve the Father Christmas story and provide years of pleasure and imagination for our children.

Free speech has cost Salman Rushdie his liberty. It is costing British Muslims many of their friends on the left of politics. It is costing the British left many of their Muslim friends. Libel damages for people like Jeffrey Archer, Elton John and Koo Stark make free speech for British newspapers very costly indeed – the going rate now is £1½ million and rising. Those who can buy a newspaper or a television station have far greater access to the so-called free marketplace of ideas than have ordinary citizens. Once the newly established Independent Television Commission has allocated its franchises, we will see the exact price of free speech through television. It will not be cheap.

Meanwhile the government tells us that the price for allowing the publication of memoirs by batty old spies is the undermining of national security and that supporters of violence in Northern Ireland cannot be allowed to speak freely on television and radio without the community paying the price in terms of outrage. In the USA, the conservative Supreme Court has recently insisted, against the better judgement of conservative politicians, that American society must pay the price for free speech even if the cost is to allow people to burn the flag or make money from dial-a-porn services. Although the former, at least, seems trivial to non-Americans, it is tantamount to blasphemy within the USA. This takes us back to Rushdie.

I want to defend free speech but I want it put in perspective. By the end of this book, I want to have convinced you that it is possible to be passionately committed to a limited but realistic concept of free speech. Sadly, the result of the current woolly argument about free speech has been a general assumption that one either has to be an absolutist free speech fanatic or an apathetic free speech cynic.

Free speech is not the most important right in the world. It is not even the most important right in world law (or, as it is more usually known, international law). It is not an absolute right. It is true that the European Convention, for example, guarantees freedom of expression in Article 10, but essential social and economic rights – for example, to food or shelter – are not mentioned. Even within the rights which the Convention does protect there are some other rights, such as Article 3 against torture, but *not* Article 10 on free speech, which are considered so fundamental that they have no exceptions and cannot under Article 15 be derogated from, even in times of war or other public emergency.

So free speech is not free, it is not the ultimate right, it is not an absolute right, it is not self-evident. Not only can it be trumped by other rights, such as privacy, it can even be outweighed by utilitarian arguments as to the general welfare of society, such as national security, under the terms of the European Convention. In the words of Article 10(2):

> The exercise of these freedoms, since it carries with it duties and responsibilities, may be subject to such formalities, conditions and restrictions or penalties as are prescribed by law and are necessary in a democratic society, in the interests of national security, territorial integrity or public safety, for the protection of disorder or crime, for the protection of health or morals, for the protection of the reputation or rights of others, for preventing the disclosure of information received in confidence, or for maintaining the authority and impartiality of the judiciary.

Hence we are not free to disregard laws on libel, official secrets, the protection of confidences, prohibitions on obscenity or racial hatred, contempt of court or copyright. The cost of disregarding these limits on free speech would be the sacrifice of other values we hold dear, such as privacy.

The thrust of this chapter has been that the way forward is to accept the power of words, that the media for conveying them have changed, and that in many ways free speech is costly. None of this means that we should weaken our commitment to a properly understood freedom of speech. It does mean, however, that we should begin by accepting that difficult, sometimes even tragic, choices have to be made between competing values.

Part II   VALUES

4   Privacy

Article 19, the international centre against censorship, has a mis-leading title, although I agree with much of its work and admire the dedication and vigour with which it has pursued its campaign for free speech. The Article 19 in question is taken from the Universal Declaration of Human Rights. It reads:

> Everyone has the right to freedom of opinion and expression; this right includes freedom to hold opinions without interference and to seek, receive and impart information and ideas through any media and regardless of frontiers.

However, its literature does not mention the limitations on this seemingly absolute right which can be found in the rest of the document and without which a completely false impression of international law is given. Thus Article 29(2) declares that:

> In the exercise of his rights and freedoms, everyone shall be subject only to such limitations as are determined by law solely for the purpose of securing due recognition and respect for the rights and freedoms of others and of meeting the just requirements of morality, public order and the general welfare in a democratic society.

It might have been more balanced to quote Article 19 of the International Covenant on Civil and Political Rights:

> (1) Everyone shall have the right to hold opinions without interference.
>
> (2) Everyone shall have the right to freedom of expression; this right shall include the freedom to seek, receive and impart information and ideas of all kinds, regardless of frontiers, either orally, in writing or in print, in the form of art, or through any other media of his choice.
>
> (3) The exercise of the right provided for in paragraph 2 of this Article carries with it special duties and responsibilities. It may

therefore be subject to certain restrictions, but these shall only be such as are provided by law and are necessary:

(a) For respect of the rights and reputations of others;

(b) For the protection of national security or of public order, or of public health or morals.

Article 20 carries further qualifications still:

(1) Any propaganda for war shall be prohibited by law.

(2) Any advocacy of national, racial or religious hatred that constitutes incitement to discrimination, hostility or violence shall be prohibited by law.

The general message from the international law of human rights seems to be that free speech sometimes conflicts with other values. Let us consider some of these clashes, that is to say, those between free speech and

(a) privacy
(b) respect for women
(c) respect for ethnic minorities
(d) respect for flags
(e) national security

In this chapter, we shall consider the conflict between free speech and privacy. Within the general rubric of privacy, there are at least two kinds of challenges to free speech. First, we might protest if lies are told about us; we might resort to libel law. Second, we might want to keep private even the truth about us, in which case we might resort to the law which protects breach of confidence.

The British press has performed a remarkable conjuring trick in this respect. It fought a long war with the government when the latter sought unsuccessfully to rely on breach of confidence to protect secrets held by Peter Wright but revealed in his book *Spycatcher*. Breach of confidence actions were represented as inimical to freedom of the press. The press then *relied* on breach of confidence claims when officers of the state, from Department of Trade inspectors to High Court judges, ordered journalists to reveal their sources.

The issue of privacy is not at the centre of these cases; they are more to do with the pragmatic considerations surrounding news gathering.

Let us instead look at a humble first instance decision of a British court which attracted relatively little publicity but is indicative of the quality of everyday journalism. Simplifying the facts somewhat, a man came home from the office one day to discover his wife in bed with another woman. He killed his wife. The other woman told another lesbian friend, in confidence, of these events. The friend later told a newspaper, which named the other woman. The criminal proceedings against the killer had not revealed the identity of his wife's lover. Could the newspaper now do so with impunity? The woman sued, requesting a court order to restrain the friend and newspaper from breaching the confidence and seeking damages for the harm already caused. The newspaper asked the court to throw the case out as disclosing no reasonable cause of action. First, the relationship was not a professional one, like that between doctor and patient. Second, even it was, the law should not protect mere tittle-tattle or trivial information. Third, even if it should, the law should not protect grossly immoral activities such as this lesbian relationship.

The judge rejected all the newspaper's claims at this stage. This did not mean that the newspaper would lose when and if the matter came to a full trial but it did mean that the woman's arguments could not be dismissed out of hand. The judge thought that the professional–client cases were not so much a category of their own as an illustration of a general point about the need to maintain confidentiality when it was implied in the relationship or when it was made an express condition as in this case. He did not think that sexual relationships could be dismissed as a mere triviality. On the contrary, they were at the core of the zone of privacy which people legitimately wished to keep to themselves. Finally, it ill behove the newspaper, which had splashed the story across its pages, to claim that the relationship was grossly immoral.

The decision was, in the light of the pre-existing law, an adventurous one. However, our concern is not with its legal credentials so much as with the moral dilemmas it opens up for free speech. Put simply, it makes us reconsider our attitude to all kinds of gossip.

The time-honoured way in which personal information becomes public property is for A to tell B in strictest confidence and on condition that it goes no further that X has done Y to or with Z. B then tells C in the very strictest confidence and on condition that C tells absolutely nobody.

And so on, and so on. The gossip-mongers claim this is just the exercise of free speech, but the cost is an invasion of privacy for X and Z. What makes it right for us to indulge in such gossip? Truth or triviality are the usual answers. The cost to the individual who is the subject of the gossip, as opposed to the cost if that person finds out that you spread the story, is rarely brought into the moral calculus.

What if the story is untrue or malicious? Nothing, is the answer for most of us. We cannot afford to pay the cost of libel lawyers and the remedy of a day in court is fraught with other costs, principally the continual republication of the libel. Nevertheless, the press are forever telling us that the cost of libel law to them is a chilling one, so that they are scared away from running stories which would serve the public interest.

Despite all the press complaints about the cost of free speech in terms of libel pay-outs, it is media figures who seem to be the ones who bring actions. For instance, Robert Maxwell is an inveterate plaintiff in libel cases. (Yes, *the* Robert Maxwell, the press magnate.) The journalist Adam Raphael has recently written an entertaining account of the absurdities of libel law, *My Learned Friends*, in which the hero, Raphael himself, seems to spend all his time involved in libel actions. In particular, he manages to sue another journalist for the way in which he reported Raphael's involvement as a witness in the most famous libel trial of recent times, the Jeffrey Archer story. The libel, interestingly enough for the subject matter of this chapter, was about Raphael's failure to maintain the absolute confidentiality of his sources by agreeing to give evidence in the Archer trial. Raphael said this was quite unfair and unrealistic. The law could have forced Raphael to tell the truth or go to prison. Moreover, given that the source had already provided his version of the conversation, Raphael felt released from the confidence. Anyway, what does a journalist do who has been libelled? Does he reply in kind by finding a journalistic outlet to put the counter-arguments? No, he goes to law and secures a deserved £45,000 settlement. Then he has the cheek to write a book about the iniquities of the current libel lottery which deters hard-hitting journalism.

As I write, the libel action dominating the headlines is the case brought by the editor of the *Sunday Times*, Andrew Neil, against the former editor of the *Sunday Telegraph*, Peregrine Worsthorne. Only a mind numbed by the constant editing of potentially libellous statements from his own newspaper would have seen the libel in the relevant article. Only a newspaper man would have risked making a public spectacle of himself by taking such an action and thus allowing other journalists to rehearse the story.

All this suggests that much of the press criticism of the libel laws is pure humbug. Once this is stripped away, much of the remaining criticism boils down to failures in legal procedure: costs are too high; damages are too high (especially when compared to the nominal sums given for more serious physical injuries) because they are set by a jury without suitable guidance from judges; and there is no appropriate procedure for a court-ordered quick apology and nominal award of damages. All these matters are simple enough to put right and need not detain us in a book about the broad ideas rather than the legal minutiae. The current reviews of the law should rectify these anomalies.

What remains as a question of principle is whether the UK should follow the example of the USA and have a different law of libel for public figures. The impact of such a change can be shown by reference to the Jeffrey Archer case. As Deputy Chairman of the Conservative Party, he would have counted as a public figure. Under American law, he would have had to demonstrate that the newspaper was motivated by malice, which would have been difficult to prove. Under English law, once he showed that the reports were defamatory, that they were likely to lower his reputation in the minds of right-thinking members of the public, then the burden was on the newspaper to prove that their allegations were true. They were unable to do so to the satisfaction of the jury.

This is relevant to our concerns because it suggests that the cost of free speech is different for public and private figures (accepting all the difficulties of drawing the line between the two). If there is a reason for easing the pressures on a newspaper in the case of a public figure it must be that the public has some greater interest in knowing about the whole life of a public person. Free speech about an individual is more important when that person might hold public office, for example, which suggests that the principal justifications for free speech might well focus on the contribution it can make to good government rather than on the idea that free speech is a good end in itself. If good government is our concern we might have less reason to worry about the cost to free speech of restrictions on pornography since that is unlikely to contribute to the democratic process. Indeed, one of the weaknesses of free speech rhetoric has been the tendency to stretch support all the way from political speech to pornographic expression, under the mistaken belief that arguments for one must apply to the other.

In the clash between free speech and privacy, the *way* in which we justify the pre-eminence of free speech is crucial. From all the foregoing arguments, the best way forward seems to be to accept that privacy should be respected unless there is a public interest at stake, such as when the plaintiff in a libel action is a figure whose trustworthiness is a matter of public concern. Why the ludicrous aspects of libel law have not been reformed is not clear, but surely part of the answer is that politicians (given their own experience at the press's hands) have no incentive to push for reform unless and until the press can be seen to be worthy of being trusted with the responsibility of exercising free speech wisely. In other words – and so back to one of our recurring themes – the press have focused on the threat to their right without realizing that the terms of the debate have moved on to consideration of the way in which the right is being used or abused. The condition upon which the law is likely to give us the liberty to libel is eternal vigilance that we use the power responsibly and we engage in dialogue as to what this means.

5 Pornography

We must, of course (and shall later) define exactly what we mean by free *speech* and freedom of *expression* in order to decide if it is accurate to describe such events as book- or flag-burning as an exercise of free speech or even of free expression. Is it not better to describe it as free burning and to shunt it off into a different intellectual category in which it can be banned without allegations of inconsistency when we bemoan other censorship? No, in my opinion, but the general point is well taken. We cannot develop a coherent account of why speech is important without developing a coherent account of what it is. Let me spoil the surprise and say that I have grave doubts as to whether pornography should come within the ambit of free speech. For the moment, however, let us suppose that it does. If we are in favour of free speech for Boris Pasternak must we also support freedom of expression for the crudest pornographer?

Here, the cost of one person's freedom may be another person's degradation; it may be the demeaning of an entire sex; it may be the direct physical assault on an identifiable individual; it may be a vague sense of disgust. It is important to clarify which cost is at issue, how seriously, and what kind of proof is being offered of the causal link between pornography and the alleged effect. The more serious the apparent cost, the more likely we are to restrict free speech and the less likely we are to require incontrovertible proof. If, for instance, a film was released around the country that appeared to lead to copy-cat rapes, many more people would be willing to have the film banned than if all that happened was that 'moral majority' campaigners picketed the cinemas.

However, the proof of the effects of pornography rarely emerges in so clearly identifiable a way. The arguments get bogged down in what causes what, whether pornography is a cause or a symptom, whether it is a problem or a solution. The 1986 Meese Report in the USA provoked much argument in this respect when it concluded that sexually violent pornography 'bears a causal relationship to anti-social acts of sexual violence and, for some subgroups, possibly unlawful acts of sexual violence'. Any veteran of free speech arguments knows how to counter this kind of assertion. The fact that both pornography and rape exist at the same time in a society does not prove anything. Violence against women occurs in societies where pornography is relatively scarce, such as Islamic countries or South Africa or Ireland, and violence against women is relatively scarce where pornography is freely available, as in Scandinavia.

Whatever the arguments for and against pornography, the reality is that all legal systems have some controls on hard-core pornography, all systems have difficulty in defining pornography in general or hard-core in particular, all definitions amount to little more than the often-quoted conclusion of US Justice Stewart: 'I may not be able to define pornography but I know it when I see it,' and all legal systems make fools of themselves from time to time through ill-judged prosecutions.

I propose to ignore all these issues, particularly since I doubt whether pornography should be brought within the compass of other free speech issues. I wish to focus instead on feminist arguments against pornography and their relevance particularly to soft-core pornography. If harm is caused to women through the availability of pornography, I suspect that the major harm is caused through the most widely available material, the magazines on sale in major newsagents and perhaps even the mass circulation newspapers, which makes arguments about hard-core material a diversion.

The feminist arguments are worth addressing not only in their own right but also because they exemplify the point made earlier that values have changed. This cost was not widely acknowledged in discussions about free speech thirty years ago. Some liberals have remained caught in a 1950s time-warp, still arguing as though the great crusade was to publish *Lady Chatterley's Lover*. Life has moved on, to the point that D. H. Lawrence's novel is sometimes criticized as sexist exploitation by some of those who once championed its publication. Vigilant against the moral majority's prudish censorship, some old-fashioned liberals have not noticed that the fundamentalist right has been joined by the feminist left. Free speech is under threat not only from those who feel that pornography degrades the sanctity of sexual expression of conjugal love but also from those who feel that it degrades women.

Feminists in the campaign against pornography seem to have had their biggest successes in North America. In Canada, a royal commission has recommended that material depicting female submissiveness should be criminalized, together with material depicting violence against women. In the USA, an ordinance in Indianapolis made it illegal to distribute material in which 'women are presented as sexual objects who enjoy pain or humiliation ... In scenarios of degradation, injury, abasement ... as sexual objects for domination, conquest, violation, exploitation, possession or use'.

This was a short-lived success since the ordinance was struck down by the courts for a variety of reasons. In US constitutional terms, it was invalid because it discriminated by not covering material which degraded men. If it were amended to deal with this point, it would still be invalid because in American law such a provision ought to judge works as a whole, and allow them redemption if they have serious literary or other artistic value. One might argue that a preferable answer to the messages being sent out by pornography is to send out counter-messages, affirming the equal dignity of the sexes, pointing out how pornography portrays women and ensuring that all are alert to the dangers of male domination being reinforced by pornography.

Perhaps learning from this experience, the current Campaign against Pornography and Censorship is concentrating less on changing the law and more on changing the attitudes of the consumers and distributors of pornography, for example through public correspondence with the largest British newsagents. Another way of putting this is to say that pressure groups are attempting to become privatized censors. The battle over soft pornography will be fought out not in the courts but in the boardroom of W. H. Smith and the women's page of the *Guardian*. I welcome this change. What worries me is that we have become so narrow in our understanding of the relevance of arguments about free speech that the rest of us will feel there is nothing to say except that it is up to W. H. Smith. Why should they forego profits if the law allows them to sell soft pornography? Why shouldn't they rely on the porno-graphers' freedom of expression?

One might as well say that the law does not force them to sell the pornography. On the other hand it does not prohibit them from selling posters which state that Father Christmas is a figment of their sales division's imagination, but that does not necessarily mean that they would be justified in doing so. It may be a free country, and it may be that W. H. Smith values free speech, but the fact is that they choose not to stock most magazines. The choice can be masked as a commercial one but it has a moral element. It is positively healthy for there to be a public debate about the merits of a company stocking or not stocking the controversial material.

What then becomes important is to have a clear sense of our own moral framework, the hierarchy of values by which we make choices. Moreover, in the world of the modern media, it is crucial to decide whether different genres of expression should be treated differently. What is suitable for a restricted viewing film is not necessarily accept-able in a mass circulation newspaper which will be seen by children. Restrictions, incidentally, are an important aspect to the debate on free speech, which too often speaks in terms of either banning or allowing. The reality is that pornography can be restricted to certain age groups or to those who are old enough and bold enough to enter special sex shops.

It is also important for us to have a sense of the surrounding culture and level of education. The more that we can be confident of a critical reception of the exploitative portrayal of stereotypes, the less demand there will be for pornography and the less impact it will have. Attempts to ban material may in effect be short-cuts to by-pass a lengthy educa-tive process. It is the culture which somehow encourages violent attitudes, rather than the pornography which feeds upon that culture, which is at the root of the problem, albeit that the two are mutually reinforcing.

By making a fuss over this omelette, feminist campaigners, in their unholy alliance with the moral majority, are engaging in the right kind of dialogue with those who make money from pornography. They are raising consciousness of, and thereby diluting, the possible impact of pornography. They are also increasing the costs of free speech for newsagents, in terms of losing public goodwill. This is the way of future debates.

6   Incitement to Racial Hatred

We have seen that Article 20 of the International Covenant on Civil and Political Rights requires states to prohibit speech that incites to certain forms of hatred. The USA has not yet ratified this treaty. Ireland has just done so and thus has been bringing its law into line with these international norms. Hence 1989 saw the first pro-gay legislation passed by the Dail, when the government accepted an amendment to its Incitement to Hatred Act – which had originally forbidden incitement on account of race, religion or nationality – so as to include sexual orientation. In the light of the previous chapter, it is worth noting that a more complex amendment backed by the Campaign against Pornography and Censorship was defeated. This would have prohibited 'hatred of women and children as portrayed in pornography', although it would not have included 'erotica', defined as sexually explicit materials premised on equality, nor bona fide sex education materials or medical or forensic literature.

But the central core of Article 20 remains the clash between free speech and protection of ethnic groups from racial hatred. One of the reasons the USA has not ratified the convention is that international law resolves this clash in favour of free speech. Even if the USA were to join the convention, it would enter a reservation on this point. Much of the rest of the world, however, balances the competing values differently. Examples could be multiplied of the international commitments to abridge free speech in the interests of racial equality, but one further illustration will suffice. Article 4 of the International Convention on the Elimination of All Forms of Racial Discrimination, which entered into force in 1969, reads in part:

> States Parties condemn all propaganda and all organizations based on ideas or theories of superiority of one race or group of persons of one colour or ethnic origin, or which attempt to justify or promote racial hatred and discrimination in any form, and undertake to adopt immediate and positive measures designed to eradicate all incitement

to, or acts of, such discrimination and, to this end, with due regard to
. . . [freedom of speech]

(a) Shall declare as an offence punishable by law all dissemination
of ideas based on racial superiority or hatred, incitement to racial
discrimination, as well as all acts of violence or incitement to such
acts against any race or group of persons of another colour or ethnic
origin, and also the provision of any assistance to racist activities,
including the financing thereof;

(b) Shall declare illegal and prohibit organizations, and also
organized and all other propaganda activities, which promote and
incite racial discrimination, and shall recognize participation in such
organizations or activities as an offence punishable by law.

No doubt the reason for the international community adopting such a
strong line against free speech where the cost is racial degradation can
be traced to our collective history, our collective repudiation of slavery
and the Holocaust. We simply do not believe that there is any possibility
that racist speech, yesterday's orthodoxy but today's heresy, will ever
become established as acceptable again. No doubt most Americans
share this view, so why will the USA not ratify the convention and
accept the other international law provisions which in effect allow
respect for racial equality to trump respect for the freedom to say the
unsayable? The cost of the USA's in many ways noble commitment to
free speech seems to be paralysis when faced with this revamped scale of
values. First Amendment absolutism ('Congress shall make no law
abridging . . . freedom of speech') antedates the Fourteenth Amendment
egalitarianism ('No state shall deny to any citizen the equal protection
of the laws . . .') by eighty years. Yet the absolutist language of the First
Amendment has been circumvented time and time again, where 'fighting
words' are concerned (a close analogy, surely), or where privacy is at
stake in defamation law, or where commercial competition is in issue
and where misleading speech could adversely affect the market. If the
will were there, a way could be found.

Perhaps the will is weakened by the traumatic memory of the Joseph
McCarthy era in the 1950s when free speech was undermined for those
of a left-wing disposition, or for those who were thought to hold such
views. Or perhaps it is fear of where to draw the line, fear that one
concession to the cost of free speech will set us sliding down the slippery

slope towards total censorship. Anticipating the argument of a later chapter, the slippery slope argument is itself slippery. As we have just seen, the American law is already on the slope, because it already allows some restrictions on free speech. The options are never simply complete freedom of speech or complete censorship.

All legal systems face the kinds of dilemma raised by the clash between free speech and respect for racial equality. Perhaps the most frequently quoted example of the tension between respecting free speech and respecting minorities is the American Skokie case. In 1978 members of the American Nazi Party wanted to march through a Jewish community in Illinois, displaying swastikas. The Illinois Supreme Court declared that the Nazis' First Amendment rights to freedom of speech were paramount and overturned a lower court's restrictions on the use of the swastikas. Controversy still rages as to whether the cost of an absolutist defence of free speech in this case was too great a burden to place on the residents of Skokie. As the intermediate court had concluded, 'the tens of thousands of Skokie's Jewish residents must feel gross revulsion for the swastika' and would be placed under intense provocation to respond in an unlawful way. Should not the law avoid this dilemma by restricting the freedom of those Nazis who had deliberately sought out a Jewish community so as to cause offence?

Fortunately, the issue of such large-scale marches does not recur frequently but a smaller scale version has recently been described as an epidemic on American campuses. How should college authorities and others respond to 'hate messages' directed at ethnic minorities, 'people of colour' in the current American terminology. In the last chapter we saw how the old-fashioned liberals who continue to use absolutist free speech rhetoric have failed to acknowledge changing values; here they are accused by Mari Matsuda and others of ignoring the cost of racist hate speech, of failing fully to appreciate the peace of mind of people of colour. She says that the typical reaction of white readers will be to dismiss tales of hate speech as isolated incidents, as 'horseplay', as nothing for which it is worth sacrificing free speech. One of the reasons why the majority sees these stories as isolated incidents is because the majority press does not report them. The ethnic minority newspapers in the USA are full of stories about harassment of Jews, Japanese, Hispanics and Blacks. The mainstream press reports the occasional invented or embellished story but neglects the real traumas. Vincent Chin, a young American of Chinese extraction, was beaten to death with baseball bats in Detroit a few years ago. His attackers were reported to have shouted words to the effect (I paraphrase their actual language) that it was because of Japanese (sic) people like him that they were out of work. The *Wall Street Journal* ran a story about background issues in 1986 headlined 'Asia bashing: bias against orientals increases with rivalry of nations' economies'. There are innumerable reported incidents of Ku Klux Klan slogans being sprayed on to garden and church walls when Blacks move into what the Ku Klux Klan thinks of as white areas. Synagogues report constant harassment – at Temple Beth Torah in Ventura, there is vandalism every few weeks, ranging from graffiti to rocks being thrown and a dead pig being left. In a case which went to court, a Black American was subjected to repeated racist speech at work, including death threats. His patience broke when a noose was left hanging one day in his work area. The attention of white liberals has finally been caught by the outbreak of such incidents on college campuses, where there have been literally hundreds of reported incidents in the last few years, such as the carving of KKK on the doors of Black students. College authorities have had to address the question of freedom for Ku Klux Klan literature. Was it acceptable for the Ku Klux Klan to distribute leaflets at Northwest Missouri State University stating that 'The Knights of the Ku Klux Klan are watching you'? Does it become unacceptable when accompanied by more specific targeting, as illustrated above?

A most impressive body of writing in American law journals by lawyers and academics of colour has castigated the attitude of white liberals to this dilemma. Free speech is exalted as a god. There is a complete failure to understand the costs to members of the attacked groups. Even though members of the self-appointed liberal élite would never dream of stooping to racist speech, neither, it seems, would they ever dream of taking legal steps to stop it.

It is fundamental to my argument that we must not only assess the costs of free speech fully and with minds open to new ways of looking at old problems, but that we must locate the debate within our own social and working lives, rather than abdicating responsibility to 'the law'. One of the ways in which public opinion and usage has changed in the United

Kingdom in the 1980s has, for instance, been through the unlikely medium of comedy, more specifically alternative comedy. This younger wave of comics has eschewed the cheap gibes and racist or sexist jokes which it associates with an older generation of British comedians. As one of the early exponents of the art, Tony Allen, put it, 'There was this drunk homosexual Pakistani squatter trade unionist takes my mother-in-law to an Irish restaurant . . . says to the West Indian waiter, "Waiter, waiter, there's a racial stereotype in my soup."' But for every alternative comic, there are many private racist jokes. Moreover, racist speech can still be heard in the public arena. Cable television in the USA has recently spawned the Diceman, a comedian who plays to a frenzied studio audience, and an increasingly large number of viewers, with old-fashioned racist jokes. In 1988 an American judge dealing with a farm worker's labour dispute was reported as telling a racist joke: 'Do you know how to make a Sp**ish omelette? Well, first you have to go out and steal three eggs.' To which counsel replied, 'I don't find ethnic jokes humorous. I don't tell them and I don't like to hear them.' Other people will regard this as hypersensitive – 'What a fuss over an omelette!' It is at this level, however, that the climate of racial equality or inequality is created. The problem of the clash between two values has been resolved by most countries against free speech. The trend is for most individuals to begin to see the force of that balance. Once we have cleaned up our own acts, there may be less need for Acts of Parliament, (although the value of such statutes in the last 25 years has been significant) but at least there will be more of a consensus behind such legal provisions as are necessary to protect racial minorities from the hostility of those recalcitrants who remain defiantly racist.

7   Flag-Waving

The British flag has been appropriated by such an odd selection of groups, ranging from the National Front to English soccer hooligans to Ulster Loyalists, that the silent majority find it difficult to summon up much emotion for the Union Jack. Although at least some of the groups think of themselves as ultra-British, the Great British public think it is decidedly un-British to make a big fuss about the flag. In the United States, however, the flag has become the nearest thing to a sacred icon that a secular state can have. Like the Queen in the UK, it is a symbol of unity and tradition. Thus many Americans react to the burning of their flag as British citizens might react to an injury done to the Queen. The same people who would be saying that freedom of expression must always be allowed, however distasteful, so that the Nazis must be permitted to march through Skokie, will be up in arms at the thought of anyone expressing themselves through burning Old Glory.

Other Americans, including a narrow majority of the present Supreme Court, believe that the constitution allows anyone to express themselves in this clearly effective way. To the amazement of foreigners, however, that recent five to four decision of the Supreme Court – in the case of Gregory Lee Johnson – was immediately challenged by the President and a clear majority of members of Congress. Chief Justice Rehnquist's impassioned dissent had evidently caught the mood of the public. Incidentally, this is one of the most remarkable legal judgments of all time, a large part of it being in verse. For example, Rehnquist not only tells us that it was the sight of the flag still flying over Fort McHenry – despite the fire of the British fleet during the war of 1812 – that inspired a Washington lawyer to scribble on the back of an envelope the poem that became the national anthem, he also gives us the verse (although not the music):

> Oh! say can you see by the dawn's early light
> What so proudly we hailed at the twilight's last gleaming?
> Whose broad stripes and bright stars, thro' the perilous fight,

O'er the ramparts we watched were so gallantly streaming?
And the rocket's red glare, the bombs bursting in air,
Gave proof thro' the night that our flag was still there.
Oh! say does that star-spangled banner yet wave
O'er the land of the free and the home of the brave?

There is much more verse and worse. It is worth noting that even Rehnquist was at pains to allow Johnson most forms of speech, however distasteful. Johnson could have said anything he liked about the flag, burned it in *private*, or burned in public effigies of political leaders or other symbols of government. In fact, Johnson did say some things about the flag which Rehnquist would have allowed. For example, 'red, white and blue, we spit on you; you stand for plunder, you will go under'. He said much about political leaders: 'Reagan, Mondale which will it be? / Either one means World War III' and 'Ronald Reagan, killer of the hour / Perfect example of US power'. So what was different about burning the flag in public? The dissenting judges thought that this had nothing to do with expressing an idea and everything to do with inciting a breach of the peace. Flag-burning was 'the equivalent of an inarticulate grunt or roar ... that was profoundly offensive'. The Texas statute which made it a criminal offence to burn the flag in public left Johnson with innumerable other ways to 'express his deep disapproval of national policy' on nuclear weapons.

The equally conservative judge, Justice Kennedy, joined the majority but felt it necessary to spell out his disapproval of what Johnson did, even if Kennedy was prepared to defend, to the death of his right-wing reputation, Johnson's right to burn the flag. The flag encapsulated the American belief in freedom, but this case 'forces recognition of the costs to which those beliefs commit us'. Here we see a judge clearly struggling to come to terms with what he described as the 'personal toll' of deciding that the constitution permits conduct of which he disapproves. Kennedy really was in the position envisaged by the apocryphal Voltaire declaration. He was also in an interesting position as a conservative. In one sense, right-wingers are seen as placing a special premium on tradition and patriotism, which would have indicated protecting the flag. In another sense, however, they are associated with a free market in all things, including ideas, and a profound distrust of governmental interference with the actions of citizens. Another conservative Reagan appointee, Justice Scalia, shared Justice Kennedy's preference for freedom when conservative values seemed to point in both directions. The other Reagan nominee, Justice Sandra Day O'Connor, joined Rehnquist, whom Reagan had appointed Chief Justice, on the other side.

The majority judgment was delivered by the arch liberal, Justice Brennan, who pointed out that as the flag had survived the bombardment at Fort McHenry, it could cope with Johnson's attentions. His conclusion conjured up the unlikely prospect of the octogenarian liberal judge honouring the burning flag by saluting and subsequently burying it, or perhaps waving his own version:

> We can imagine no more appropriate response to burning a flag than waving one's own, no better way to counter a flag-burner's message than by saluting the flag that burns, no surer means of preserving the dignity even of a flag that burned than by – as one witness here did – according its remains a respectful burial. We do not consecrate the flag by punishing its desecration, for in doing so we dilute the freedom that this cherished emblem represents.

Others might feel that it is as silly to bury the remains of a flag as it is to burn it in the first place. What is important for our purposes is that both sides take the issue so seriously when, to those of us from a different culture, it seems unbelievable that a system which places such store by free speech that it will not prohibit racist expressions of hate can nevertheless agonize over the cost of the freedom to burn a flag. This is not to sneer at American patriotism but to draw the attention of American readers to the fact that absurd debates about the cost of free speech in British law, such as blasphemy, have their parallel in what seem to outsiders to be absurd debates on the other side of the Atlantic. Nor would I wish to underestimate the emotive power of flags. In Northern Ireland, it was for many years regarded as illegal to fly the Irish tricolour and while today it is legal to do so, the provocative use of both tricolours and loyalist flags can be regulated. A Protestant employer is not free to drape Union Jacks all over his workplace as a way of intimidating Catholic employees or potential employees, nor can a Republican employer use the Irish tricolour in similar fashion to deter Protestant workers.

Symbols can of course wield tremendous power and their use or misuse has serious implications for freedom of expression. Even if we conclude with the Supreme Court majority that free speech wins the day, we can recognize that others regard this as a high price to pay for liberty. A subsidiary reason for referring to this recent Supreme Court decision is that Justice Brennan wisely quotes the perceptive comments of one of his predecessors, Justice Brandeis, who observed in a 1927 case that

> To courageous, self-reliant men, with confidence in the power of free and fearless reasoning applied through the processes of popular government, no danger flowing from speech can be deemed clear and present, unless the incidence of the evil apprehended is so imminent that it may befall before there is opportunity for full discussion. If there be time to expose through discussion the falsehood and fallacies, to avert the evil by the processes of education, the remedy to be applied is more speech, not enforced silence.

This passage repays careful study. The assumptions in it are significant, of popular government, of confidence in the openness to reason. The preferred solution is undeniably the best way forward, to counter speech with better speech. In particular, education is at the heart of the matter. On the other hand, there is the inference that censorship may be the lesser of two evils if there is no time in which to build up an appropriate culture of verbal challenge to verbal challenge. This sense that legal restrictions are at most second best is vital to those who value free speech. Censorship is an unattractive short-cut, to be used with reluctance when the cost of untrammelled freedom is too high, but to be replaced with voluntary restraint whenever possible.

8   Official Secrets

The bizarre *Spycatcher* saga involved worldwide litigation and near-universal condemnation of the British government and British judges. Even British judges were criticizing British judges in outspoken terms. As one of the dissenting Law Lords, Lord Bridge, said in the first *Spycatcher* case: 'freedom of speech is always the first casualty under a totalitarian regime'. He felt that the government and majority judges were taking a 'significant step down that very dangerous road'. The government would, he claimed, face 'inevitable condemnation and humiliation by the European Court of Human Rights in Strasbourg'.

The majority disagreed. In the first case, they were prepared to grant the government an interim injunction to prevent newspapers publishing Peter Wright's allegations until the full trial. Lord Ackner saw 'no prospect of the Convention availing' the press. He talked of 'press hysteria', their reaction to the litigation amounted to an abuse of power and was a depressing reflection of falling standards. He asked whether critics in the press would like the law to become a jellyfish rather than a rock. Lord Ackner said that the judicial cry for a sense of proportion went 'totally unheeded by the entire media'. He asked for but a 'tithe' of the publicity given to the ill-formed criticisms to be accorded to the basis of the judgement and the reasons given.

Lord Templeman was very careful to emphasize that he was deciding in a democratic framework, in accordance with his reading of the UK's international commitments. He pointed out that Article 10 of the European Convention which declares a right of freedom of expression, including a right to a free press, accepts restrictions on free speech if they are 'necessary' in the interests of, for example, national security, the protection of information received in confidence, and to maintain the authority and impartiality of the judiciary.

By the time of the second *Spycatcher* case, however, the Law Lords were convinced that the restrictions were not really 'necessary'. The European Court of Human Rights interprets 'necessary' to require 'a pressing social need'. Since *Spycatcher* was widely available all over the world, the government was unlikely to convince the court that the information within it remained confidential, so it argued at the full trial that the real public interest was in stopping future memoirs by other spies. This did not amount to a pressing reason for preventing newspaper coverage of this memoir. The Law Lords held in favour of the press. Freedom of speech had defeated the government's claims, albeit after a long hard struggle. This is not the place for a detailed account of the judicial attitude.

What is significant, however, is that the British government's obsession with secrecy became an international amusement as it sent lawyers around the globe in the vain quest for the grail of a permanent injunction. The better strategy would have been to have treated the book with the indifference it deserved from the outset rather than give it worldwide publicity, thereby turning a dreary and unpromising publication into an international bestseller. American readers could tell from the opening account of the geography of Washington DC that Peter Wright was not a reliable guide to anything. As Geoffrey Robertson QC, a civil liberties lawyer, has observed, Wright's paranoia was more worrying than any of his so-called revelations (which Wright later admitted were exaggerated):

the real public interest in this book lay not in its accusations against Hollis (which even Wright's co-author has rejected) but in what it revealed about the mentality of its author, and the standards within MI5 which allowed people with that mentality to occupy positions of power outside any legal or democratic control.

Another point of importance in the *Spycatcher* saga is the way in which the British legal system was castigated as inferior in its respect for free speech to all manner of foreign courts and in particular the US Supreme Court. That court's reputation may come from the Pentagon Papers case in which it ruled that 'prior restraint' of official secrets was not an option it would allow the US government unless lives would be lost. But there are many ways of inhibiting free speech and the record of the two jurisdictions is not so radically divergent. After all, the British press ultimately won the *Spycatcher* case.

In the USA, in 1980, the Supreme Court ordered a CIA agent, Frank Snepp, to give to the government all his profits from a book about the

CIA's involvement in the Vietnam War, *Decent Interval*. What is more extraordinary, it did not even grant Snepp the opportunity to put his case before it rejected the remedy proposed by the appellate court and restored the lower court's draconian ruling.

In 1988, four days after the British Law Lords decided against the government in the *Spycatcher* case, the US Supreme Court made another anti-free speech decision by refusing to overturn the criminal conviction of a US government employee, Samuel Morison, who had leaked classified information (about explosions in Soviet naval bases, as it happens) to the British journal *Jane's Defence Weekly*. Even if the information had not been classified, the decision would have been the same. For good measure, the US government was, at the same time as prosecuting leakers, putting forward legislation to Congress requiring the death penalty for those who leak even unclassified information to any third party.

Meanwhile, back in the UK, the government was similarly determined to clamp down on revelations from former spies and leaks from other 'moles'. Hence it responded to its *Spycatcher* defeat with its 1989 new Official Secrets Act, which gave itself a dazzling array of powers to suppress free speech. In particular, the new act has no 'public interest' defence for those who leak, nor for those who publish such leaks in the press or elsewhere.

The message is, therefore, that governments everywhere have taken extraordinary steps to protect 'official secrets', almost regardless of the significance of those 'secrets'. This is a scattershot approach which carries many costs for free speech. Nobody could sensibly deny the need to keep some governmental information secret. For example, the civil liberties lobby, so often on the side of free speech, was quite rightly the first to condemn those members of the security forces in Northern Ireland who were alleged in 1989 to have leaked to loyalist paramilitaries information about the identity of suspected republican paramilitaries. Nobody in their right mind believes that the cost of a free trade in such information is a price worth paying. On the other hand, surely nobody could deny that some 'secrets' are only kept confidential to save the government from embarrassment rather than to save the country from a genuine threat to national security. Moreover, the culture of secrecy prevents citizens from having access to exactly the kind of information a political justification for free speech would claim needs to be circulated.

There is much to be said for the kind of Freedom of Information Act they have in such countries as Australia, Canada, France, New Zealand and the USA. The basic idea of this varying legislation is to establish the right of public access to all official information bar that which can be justifiably exempted, the details of which categories can be excluded and who should decide again varying. The absence of such information severely circumscribes the freedom of the press to speak out against the government of the day. At any rate, the possibilities of such acts are shown by the experience of many other legal systems. The common lesson is once again that the debate about the clash between free speech and national security is not an all-or-nothing competition. Lines will have to be drawn. The central questions are where, and by whom?

The answers are all too obvious at the descriptive level and all too difficult at the normative level. That is to say, it is clear that governments draw the lines in their own interest, but what is not clear is who else could or should draw the line and what other standard should be substituted. To the extent that many government decisions are challengeable in the courts, one might argue that judges ought to have the last word but their record has not been exemplary and they themselves seem to think that the executive is best placed to decide. I would argue strongly for a test of what is in the public interest, as distinct from what is in the interest of the political party who happen to be in government. What is in the public interest is not to be identified, as judges often remind us, with what interests or titillates the public. There is every reason to expect that such a test would still yield more freedom of information than would the present culture of secrecy.

Such information is needed not just for the debates about spy-catching, which have always seemed rather remote to me, but for such controversies as those surrounding Messrs Stalker and Wallace in Northern Ireland. Disinformation and secrecy can only be countered by investigative reporting and alternative information. Governments must expect a critical reaction from the press and others so long as their first instinct is to distrust the public's ability to appreciate the true reasons for action. Some of the media's finest hours, most notably Watergate in the USA, have involved the dogged use of free speech to uncover public scandals, and we have every reason to oppose strongly government moves to inhibit such investigations. This is a clash between values in which free speech must triumph in all but the rare cases where national security or the personal safety of individuals is truly at stake.

The inevitable conclusion is that we often simply do not believe the claims which governments, of all nations and political hues, advance to inhibit free speech. This is an example of the irresponsible use of a counter-value – national security or official secrecy – weakening respect for its core significance. Too often, the boot has been on the other foot, with the press forfeiting our confidence through indiscriminate use of free speech rhetoric, as in the conflict with privacy – the tussle with which we began Part II. As we end our initial look at some reports from the battlegrounds of free speech, the overriding impression is of bad arguments driving out the good ones. In the next chapter, we make some efforts to sort out the good from the bad and the downright ugly.

Part III   ARGUMENTS

Now that we are aware of some of the clashes between free speech and other values, it is time to take stock of the kinds of arguments we all use in deciding whether free speech should prevail. In this chapter, we will look at some of the most common cheap gibes and debating tricks, the slippery arguments like the slippery slope. Once the bad arguments have been identified and removed, we should be able to make some progress towards a more constructive analysis of free speech.

The slippery slope argument is used as a trump card in so many debates on free speech issues that it is often assumed to be a clinching move when it is in fact far from convincing. The imagery is powerful. It assumes we are at the top of a slope with absolute free speech. Once we set foot on the slope of censorship by banning, for example, racist speech, then we will inevitably slide down the hill towards complete oppression, banning Shakespeare or banning speech which teases short people. So let's not risk sliding down the slope however high the cost of free speech in this instance.

Curiously enough, in the very home of the slippery slope argument for absolutist views of free speech, the liberal state of Massachusetts in the USA, the people of Boston managed to leap to the bottom of the slope without taking the initial step of prohibiting racist speech. Incredibly, Boston banned a song by Randy Newman called 'Short People', the lyrics of which indicated that 'short people got no reason to live'. In words which Salman Rushdie was to echo a decade later, Newman explained that he had been misunderstood; he was trying to show how absurd all prejudice was by taking a far-fetched example. He did not mean to insult short people. Missing the irony, or disbelieving the singer/songwriter, campaigners and politicians did more to defend short people from the alleged hurt they were feeling than they have hitherto achieved for people of colour who suffer more pernicious discrimination of a wholly different order. Looking at the issue in reverse, one could say that history shows that one ban does not necessarily lead to another. The short song ban was short-lived. If it is seen as the first step down a slippery slope, there has been no more slip.

The fact is that we are never at the top of the slope; we are always holding a position somewhere on the hill. It is extremely misleading to pretend that we are at the top of the hill when there are dozens of laws which already (usually with justification in terms of some other cost) restrict free speech. There are laws on patents, copyright, contracts in restraint of trade, protection of trade secrets, intellectual property, misleading or dangerous advertisements and consumer protection, libel, slander, treason, conspiracy to commit crimes, official secrets, breach of confidence and obscenity, to name a few. In many of these areas the law has been stable for many years or sometimes in retreat back up the hill. There is no automatic slide to more censorship. On the contrary, to those people of colour who are trying to invoke the protection of the law from racist hate speech, it must seem as if they are at the bottom of a slippery slope and facing the task of walking *up* the hill.

This version of the slippery slope has been described as the 'horrible results' claim: do not take this step, however desirable it may seem, because it will lead to a horrible result. An alternative argument has been dubbed the 'arbitrary results' claim: do not ban this unless you can justify distinguishing it from that which you do not want to ban. In popular parlance, where are you going to draw the line? How can you ban hard-core pornography unless you can draw a bright line between it and soft pornography? This misconceives the way in which the law, or our personal judgement on free speech, develops. We do not have to draw the line once and for all in advance of any contested cases. We can allocate examples as they occur to one or other category, and accept that some are borderline or hard cases, without doubting that others deserve to be on one or other side of the line. Just because a man with a limited amount of hair trailed across his head might be called bald by one person and not bald by another, does not mean that it is impossible to assign Yul Brynner to one side of the line and Harrison Ford to the other. It does not invalidate the concept of baldness to note that there will be difficulties of adjudication. Simi-larly, while there may be other arguments against banning hard-core pornography, this is not a good one. In the real world, what seems to be the most arbitrary line can have a rationale. It may be difficult to distinguish driving at 29 miles per hour from driving at 31 miles per hour, but it makes sense to draw the line at 30 miles per hour for ease of recognition.

In relation to free speech, it is one of the most slippery tactics to rely on the slippery slope, yet it is the first instinct of so many debaters, particularly in relation to the issues discussed in the preceding chapters. This is not to deny that one form of censorship can sometimes lead to another but it is to say that it is not inevitable that it will. Another dubious tactic is name-calling: 'You would say that, wouldn't you, because you're a liberal/conservative/woman/man/black/white/Muslim/Christian.' This is designed to undermine the position of the opponent by representing it as self-interested. Again, there is a tendency for it to work against minorities who cannot find others to stand up for their rights and who are therefore always likely to be vulnerable to this attack. There are several disturbing features of this dismissal. It ignores the merits of the arguments about free speech and it stereotypes people. It is just plain wrong to imply that all Muslims think alike on the Rushdie issue or that all conservatives agree on what to do about flag-burning (ask Justices Scalia and Rehnquist).

Next comes the attempt to win the free speech debate through the use of morally loaded language, by using such terms as 'censorship' or 'licence'. We should be alert to see whether we really accept them as the best description of whatever is in issue. Another form of this sort of argument is being used when we hear that there is no point in banning, say, pornography because the law will only drive the free speech underground. There may be an element of truth in this anxiety, but in fact the law never succeeds in banning anything completely.

Finally, we are all quick to accuse one another of inconsistency. This charge has been my stock-in-trade so far: how can writers defend Rushdie's free speech and at the same time attack the freedom of Bradford Muslims to express their revulsion at the book? Isn't that inconsistent? So I am as guilty as the next person in alleging inconsistency. Yet I realize that there are two good responses to such a charge. First, it might be argued that the two instances are not inconsistent. Subtle differences may have eluded the accuser. Second, an inconsistency might be admitted but the counter would be to insist that we cannot be consistent across the range of tragic choices. The only way in which society can come to terms with its conflicting values is to prefer one value in some circumstances and another in different conditions. When should free speech triumph?

10   What Is Speech?

The previous Part laid out, in successive chapters, the values which are most frequently cited as being in competition with free speech. But what exactly is speech if it encompasses such activities as burning a flag and displaying a swastika?

This question is particularly important for judges who are interpreting a constitution which guarantees freedom of speech, but it is not so troublesome for us, since our primary concern is not legal. We need only pause briefly, then, to consider the American constitutional position. In the flag-burning case, Justice Brennan began by observing that, 'The First Amendment literally forbids the abridgement only of "speech", but we have long recognized that its protection does not end at the spoken or written word.' Speech does not simply mean speech. Speech in this sense has something to do with the communication of ideas, which could easily be achieved by a picture. The American understanding of speech in its constitutional sense is that it connotes an intention to convey a message with a likelihood that the message would be understood. It covers assertions of fact and value, not only in the public arena of politics but also in the private discourse of one's home (not that that is usually under threat of censorship). What, then, is the distinction between speech and conduct? Burning a flag might be described as speech under the expansive approach – but is it not more clearly conduct? Or, to vary the theme, although bombing the Grand Hotel in Brighton carried a message as to the IRA's opinion about the British government, was it enough to turn conduct into speech?

For our purposes, a broad concept of expression is the better starting-point. We could argue that freedom of speech is absolute because pornography is not speech, racist messages are not speech, flag-burning is not speech, and so on, but then this chapter on defining what counts as speech would have to expand to fill the entire book. We would be concealing arguments of substance within arguments of definition. Unless there is a compelling reason to do otherwise, namely the demands of a constitutional legacy, it is better to cast the net widely and catch big fish as well as small.

At the central core of our concerns will come political speech, such as criticism of government policies, because there are additional reasons to protect it than there are for pornography, which remains at the penumbra of the concept of speech. For both political dissent and pornography, we can claim justifications like respecting the autonomy of individuals; but for political dissent we can claim an extra reason, its contribution to the running of a democracy, which cannot so plausibly be invoked on behalf of pornography.

One weakness of many discussions of free speech is the pretence that any argument for freedom of expression must apply across the board. This just dilutes the value of the democracy defence of political speech. Nor should we pretend that the various justifications for free speech have the intensity or strength in all cases to which they do apply.

Once these points are accepted, and it is also admitted that the value challenging free speech will be different for different examples of speech, then a realistic, if complex picture begins to appear. What emerges is that the threshold question, 'is it expression?', quickly gives way to the more important inquiry, 'why is this kind of speech valuable?', so that when we reach the next question, 'what is the strength of any countervailing cost of this free speech?', we have uncovered the true values at stake.

If on the other hand we set great store by the preliminary question, 'is it speech or conduct?', the answer is that flag-burning and similar activity could be brought under either rubric and how we view it will be inextricably linked with whether or not we want to protect it. If we somehow believe that speech is special, is more worthy of protection than mere conduct, then there will be a great temptation to place behaviour in one or other category to achieve a desired result.

As it happens, I *do* believe that most of us are influenced by the belief that there is a crucial difference between speech and action, although I am less convinced that the distinction is universally valid. One reason for supporting free speech is the assumption that it is less harmful than action. It is obviously harmful to attack physically a member of an ethnic minority (or anyone else), but it is often claimed that it is not harmful to attack them verbally. The truth is that it *is* harmful to attack them verbally, depending on one's definition of harm, but it is generally less damaging. This generalization, however, may be defeated in a particular instance. Moreover, it is true to say that we cannot go through life without having our sensibilities offended. We must expect, and we will certainly encounter, some such harms along the way, insults being a prime example.

What counts as speech worthy of protection will vary from society to society and from time to time, within a society, but a realistic assessment of our commitment to free speech must include looking at the way in which it is used. Whether art is pornography and whether under either heading it counts as speech is not a semantic point, to be resolved by dictionary definitions, it is an issue that is never resolved without the spectre of censorship hanging over the classification.

In my view, therefore, it is not a particularly productive use of our energies to construct a narrow definition of speech. I would prefer the broader term of freedom of expression, although in the title of this book, and often in the text, I bow to popular (more concise) usage. Moreover, the wonders of modern science are constantly bringing us new media of expression, so that those discussions of free speech which take as their unarticulated premise that we are dealing with the freedom to address a public meeting at Hyde Park Corner, or to run off a pamphlet on a printing press, need to be jolted out of their time-warp.

Tobacco advertising is a case in point. The cigarette companies have been forced by governments to carry health warnings on their promotional material. There has been little outcry against this form of enforced or dictated speech. Against the day when governments go further and ban all 'speech' in favour of the freedom to smoke, tobacco companies have sought to develop an identification between their brands and a particular colour, image or object. Thus Silk Cut becomes associated with purple silk, suitably cut. The colour can then be used as the background to hoardings at sporting events sponsored by Silk Cut, so as to circumvent any censorship. Is the colour any less 'speech' than a picture or a slogan? Interestingly, few civil libertarians seem at all troubled by the way in which governments have reduced the freedom of expression of tobacco companies, first banning advertising on television, then dictating the terms of other advertising, and so on. As a non-smoker, I am not at all eager to defend to the death the rights of tobacco companies to make money by cultivating other people's ill-health, but if I were, I would not expect the debate to be conducted in terms of what is speech, so much as in terms of what is acceptable and unacceptable. This is not to say that we should ignore the distinctive aspects of free speech and subsume its value within the general rallying cry of freedom.

But we must reflect on whether freedom of speech has a distinct role as compared with other freedoms. Can we justify free speech independently of justifying liberty in general? I think that the question is misconceived. We do not have liberty so much as specific liberties. This is illustrated for lawyers by the way in which constitutions like the US Bill of Rights or the provisions of the European Convention on Human Rights separate out different liberties. The kinds of reasons advanced will be similar but not identical. There is not some single special magical explanation of freedom of speech which does not apply to freedom of thought or freedom of assembly or freedom of religion or freedom to vote or freedom from arbitrary arrest. These freedoms are interconnected, albeit each with a distinct role to play. Each has a contribution to make to the culture in which we may flourish. There are many reasons for respecting all these liberties. We do not have to pick one unifying theme. This would be to oversimplify a complex reality in which values conflict.

If we refuse to get caught in the game of defining speech too narrowly and if we refuse to indulge in the poor arguments, where should we find the best arguments? What has emerged from the discussions of value conflicts?

If we choose free speech in preference to competing values we are supported by three powerful reasons. First, by the claim that it is an essential part of the democratic process. Second, emphasis is sometimes placed on the idea that it is a vital adjunct to the autonomous life. How can we develop as human individuals if we do not have the opportunity to debate, to give and to receive information and ideas? Third, it is often said that free speech is the surest route towards the emergence of truth, so that today's heresy might become tomorrow's orthodoxy.

It has become part of liberal dogma that these reasons are inviolate and interrelated. It is true that one or all of them can underpin any particular claim of free speech, but it is not true that they all relate to all speech. Nor is it true that all speech can measure up to these claims. For example, who really believes that racist hate messages might prove to be 'true'? In what way do they contribute to the democratic process? If it is essential for the autonomous life to be able to say racist things and hear racist slogans, then why exactly is autonomy such a desirable end-in-itself?

The doubts about the best justifications for free speech are not new. John Stuart Mill has often been criticized for a lack of clarity as to the basis of his commitment to freedom of expression. Was he defending free speech as an end-in-itself or because he believed that it could be justified on a utilitarian calculus as contributing to the general welfare of society? What has happened recently is that in the face of outrageous threats to free speech from the Ayatollah Khomeini and elsewhere, we have abandoned our methodological differences and united under the common banner of free speech, trusting to the mythology of the slippery arguments and hoping that others will not spot the weak links in our reasoning.

This is understandable but regrettable, for free speech is facing new dilemmas, not only through the threat from sophisticated worldwide terrorism but also from the power that new forms of mass media offer to their controllers. How can we decide on the answer to a new problem, such as whether Rupert Murdoch is entitled to use his newspapers to bolster his satellite television company, unless we have a firm grasp of our justifications for free speech?

Moreover, moral philosophy is moving on from the days when the media pundits were at university and learnt that there were two alternative world views, rights theories and varieties of utilitarianism. The language that opinion-formers adopt is still based on these views. It must be said that they are not always consistent in their reasoning. In relation to the current debate on embryo experiments, for example, they will use utilitarian arguments that the general welfare to be gained from developing in vitro fertilization and perhaps eradicating hereditary diseases must trump any rights which ought otherwise to be accorded to the early embryo. In the free speech arena, however, utility is abandoned to the dogma of inalienable, absolute rights.

In fact, it is perfectly plausible to support or oppose embryo experiments or free speech from either a utilitarian or a rights-based perspective. One could argue, for example, as to when rights holders come into being and deal with the embryo problem in that way. The perception remains that liberal commentators are utilitarians dressed, when it suits them, in rights clothing and that they have little sense even of where to look for sophisticated analysis of the underlying moral questions. They chip away at their square peg utilitarianism until it (just about) fits the round hole of a right to free speech, instead of looking at new materials and tools.

These could be found in the increasing willingness of moral philosophers to question the choice as posed between utilitarianism and rights. On the one hand, we have the theory that utility, or the balance of pleasure over pain caused by an action, is the touchstone. This seems to reflect the pragmatism of political compromise but fails to recognize the inviolability of certain interests. Thus, surely the Holocaust would have been wrong however much the Nazis enjoyed torture and genocide, and however stoical were their victims? Moreover, how can we gather the evidence for such a utilitarian calculus? For these and other reasons, principally the accusation that utilitarianism treats people as means rather than as ends in themselves, a rival theory of dignity for human individuals has been developed, often expressed in Kantian rhetoric about treating people always as ends in themselves and never merely as means, which is much quoted but seldom understood. Splendid, but who has the resulting rights, and what is their content? Respect does not help us to find decisive answers to free speech questions. Rights may conflict. And why should a weak right trump a strong non-right? If utilitarianism is too malleable, rights talk is too rigid.

One solution to this disagreement is to improve on either theory until it becomes convincing. Others are to look for a third way or to stop looking for a master-plan ethical framework but to accept that different individuals have different moral values and that part of the human condition is to argue endlessly about such conflicts. The second and third options seem more attractive to me. I believe that we do have different moral values, that even for an individual, let alone a society, such values can conflict, and that we are thus faced with tragic choices. Hence inconsistency in a legal system is sometimes a virtue rather than a vice, reflecting our uncertainty and unwillingness to defeat one conscientiously held view time after time. This is very much the case with free speech. I have argued that it clashes with other values and that societies will resolve the conflict differently according to the context. An oppressive legal system will allow free speech only for its own supporters and will attack oppressed groups. A more democratic system might be more willing to defend a disadvantaged group from harsh speech by others. A utopian society would not need to restrict free speech because its members would respect one another instinctively and would be self-confident enough as to their standing in society not to take umbrage at imagined slights.

If we are to look for a way out of the philosophical impasse of rights v. utility, however, then there are other ways of approaching such moral dilemmas as those involving free speech. In particular, Professor Joseph Raz, has argued in a characteristically difficult but brilliant book, *The Morality of Freedom*, that the foundations of morality include values other than rights, such as duties, goals and virtues. Raz uses as an example the case of owning a Van Gogh painting, and thus having the right to destroy it. Raz believes that we should not stop our moral analysis at this point, nor need we collapse into utilitarianism in arguing that we should preserve the painting. Raz argues that it makes moral sense to say that I am under a duty to preserve the painting because 'to destroy it and to deny the duty is to do violence to art and to show oneself blind to one of the values which give life a meaning'. It is an impoverished vision of the human condition to imagine that the only value is utility or that all interests can be divided into rights and non-rights, with the latter weighing next to nothing.

Raz places great store by the autonomous life, the ability to choose from a range of options a way of living which one values, indeed which reflects one's values. This requires a more positive view of government than is often provided by other liberal thinkers. Instead of thinking about free speech in terms of the absence of censorship, for example, no doubt Raz would argue that the government must take positive action to create a culture in which free speech can flourish. As he observes:

> The doctrine of limited government regards governments as a threat to liberty. Its protection is in keeping governments confined within proper moral bounds. While not denying that governments can and often do, pose a threat to individual liberty, there is another conception which regards them also as a possible source of liberty. They can create conditions which would enable their subjects to enjoy greater liberty than they otherwise would. This second conception regards liberty as sometimes threatened by individuals and corporations, not only by governments. It goes further and claims that though governments sometimes abuse their powers and trespass on individual liberty, in situations which are not all that rare they should act to promote freedom, and not only sit back and avoid interfering with it. ... Freedom [is] a distinct value, but one which is intimately intertwined with others, and cannot exist by itself.

Compulsory primary and secondary education is an example of government intervention which restricts our freedom to play truant to enhance our powers of autonomy in the long run. Most obviously in relation to free speech, it is important to develop literacy and preferably critical faculties before it becomes meaningful to talk of free speech enhancing our lives. Raz's last point, about the interdependence of freedom and other values, such as respect for the equal dignity of other human individuals, is one which finds many echoes in this book. If the government and individuals work for better relationships between religious groups, for example, this will in turn enhance the freedom of scope for writers and others to criticize those religions. But justification for free speech, like freedom itself, cannot make sense in a moral vacuum.

The best justifications for freedom of expression, then, are those which acknowledge the variety of moral values at stake and then pinpoint the distinctive contribution speech can offer. Of the three arguments outlined above, the development of personal autonomy might seem to be the one which best fits the Raz framework. It is important to experiment, to say what one thinks, to hear what others think, otherwise one is not truly autonomous. Quite so, but autonomy is not, it seems to me, an all-or-nothing value. There are degrees of autonomy and there are some degrees not worth having. If one person's autonomy conflicts with another's self-dignity, then some value systems would prefer a world in which the first person's autonomy is restricted. Indeed, this is Raz's preference: 'autonomy-based freedom ... does not extend to the morally bad and repugnant. Since autonomy is valuable only if it is directed at the good it supplies no reason to provide, nor any reason to protect, worthless let alone bad options.' What we ought to be looking for is a multiplicity of *valuable* options, and favourable conditions in which to choose between them. That is what pluralism ought to be about, not about the provision of endless degrading options. Of course, this leaves us back in a moral quandary of how we identify the morally valuable from the pernicious, but nobody pretended that a realistic ethical structure would make life easy.

My own view is that this is where the other justifications come into their own. It *is* difficult to be confident of the criteria by which one dismisses hard-core pornography as not providing a valuable option, even if I, for one, am prepared to put racist hate speech firmly in this category, but where speech relates to the criticism of governments or ideologies, then without knowing any more about the substance of the speech, I would deem it valuable. If speech might plausibly lead to better government or to the 'truth', then orthodoxy deserves to be challenged. This does not quite make such speech inviolable. Its form could be so abusive as to cause other problems, or it might be associated with violence to such an extent that its initial privileged status is indefensible. As a general rule, these traditional justifications are most persuasive when providing options from which to choose valuable political or religious or other beliefs.

It follows that I would warn against an attempt to choose one of these three lines of argument as the exclusive justification of free speech, and I would also warn against stretching them too far. In particular, it seems to me to weaken respect for the arguments about better government and tomorrow's orthodoxy to claim that they have some relevance to hard-core pornography or to racist hate speech. They do not.

Furthermore, I would warn against excessive reflection on these abstract arguments in isolation from concrete problems of free speech. The best way forward is to apply the Rawlsian framework to these and other moral dilemmas. The American political philosopher, John Rawls, has urged us to be aware of our intuitive responses to such questions and then to test our intuitions by constructing moral theories. If the intuitions do not stand up to the test, then modify the intuitions or the test. In this way, one can reach a 'reflective equilibrium'. Now, I have already indicated that I doubt whether society as a whole will agree on the point of equilibrium, but the process is nonetheless a valuable one. There are any number of ways of testing your intuitions about free speech, and the need to think at a principled level and in relation to specific problems is one reason for the structure of this book, which moves between the particular and the general. But Rawls's own test is perhaps the best way of examining our intuitions honestly.

Imagine you are coming together with your fellow citizens to lay down the ground rules for your society, but that you are operating under a veil of ignorance. You are under instructions to decide in your own best interests but the veil has obscured who your 'self' is. You might be the Ayatollah Khomeini or Rushdie, a pornographer or a rape victim, white or black, a pop star or an investigative journalist. On what principles would you organize a moral and legal structure of free speech? In the real world our awareness of our self-interest makes many discussions of free speech lead nowhere. We expect publishers and the press to take up one position, governments and fundamentalist terror-ists others. The attempt, at least, would be worthwhile, on a second reading of the examples discussed in this book. How convincing are the three arguments from under the veil?

There is really little more to say about the good arguments in abstract. For the reality is that each of these three justifications might have a role to play, that all three of them together might not be sufficient to outweigh some other value, that the parts they have to play will vary from issue to issue, culture to culture, time to time. In other words, the failure of most discussions of free speech begins with the adoption of such catch-phrases wrenched from any context and then applied with fundamentalist fervour.

The better way forward is to seek to understand the surrounding story whenever we feel that free speech is under threat. This is often a signal that something else is wrong within our social or political fabric. Hence the next two sections tell the stories of particular sagas at greater length. The purpose of this brief chapter has been to sweep away false hopes that the dilemmas we encountered earlier can be resolved through some rhetorical trickery, or definitional game-playing, or global solutions. It is actually easy to grasp the main thrust of the free speech arguments. What is difficult is to be sure that we understand the dispute to which we bring those arguments. The most talked about but least understood Great Debates on free speech of recent vintage are the Rushdie affair and the Sinn Fein television ban, to which we now turn.

Part IV   SALMAN RUSHDIE
             AND
             THE SATANIC VERSES

Salman Rushdie's book, *The Satanic Verses*, was published in the UK on 26 September 1988, banned in India on 5 October, banned in South Africa on 24 November and banned in Iran on 15 February 1989, together with all Viking/Penguin books. On 14 February, Ayatollah Khomeini had issued his notorious *fatwa* on Rushdie.

Several people were killed in riots in Bombay and Kashmir, several bookstores in the United Kingdom were bombed, many bookstores around the world, particularly in the USA, withdrew copies for a time in the face of death threats to employees. Rushdie himself went into hiding, protected by the British government and police. This was ironic since his protectors had themselves been severely criticized in the book. One of the characters, Saladin, is beaten up in a police van and an effigy of the Prime Minister, referred to as Mrs Torture, is burnt.

Reaction *to* the book fulfilled expectations *in* the book. Islam was seen to be intolerant, one of the premises of the book. The prophetic words of Mahound were echoed by the Ayatollah: 'Your blasphemy, Salman, can't be forgiven. Did you think I wouldn't work it out? To set your words against the Words of God ... ' Rushdie explained, in an open letter to Rajiv Gandhi, the Indian Prime Minister, that the book was not about Islam but about 'migration, metamorphosis, divided selves, love, death, London and Bombay'. He relied on the fact that the book was fiction. Others felt that they did not have to be the most sophisticated of literary critics to allow that this fiction could be interpreted as a distorted view of the facts. Still others said that it did not matter whether the work was represented as fiction or not, no writer was entitled to talk about sacred matters in such profane language.

Muslims objected to the name Mahound – which means false prophet – being attributed to a prophet-like figure who is also an unscrupulous, lecherous man (and in no way divine). They were appalled by the idea that this figure would have included in the Koran the satanic verses suggested by the devil. Mahound is represented as dominating his followers by inspiring fear. A brothel sequence in which the prostitutes are named after the Prophet's twelve wives was regarded by Muslims as deeply offensive.

Rushdie continued to emphasize that this was a work of fiction and that, in so far as it had a message, it was one which applied to all religions and in particular to the fundamentalist strands of religions. He took an absolutist line on free speech: 'Everything is worth discussing. There are no subjects which are off limits and that includes God, includes prophets.' Muslim critics responded by saying that there was a time and a place and a style and a manner for most things but that there was no licence to use such degrading language about what they took to be the core of their faith.

One of the recurring charges against Muslims from Bombay to Bradford was that they had not read what they were condemning. In response one writer graphically observed in what amounted to an open letter to Rushdie, published by the *Times of India*: 'I do not have to wade through a filthy drain to know what filth is. My first inadvertent step would tell me what I have stepped into. For me, the synopsis, the review, the excerpts, your gloatings were enough.'

For our purposes, it is essential to place all this in perspective. Hostile reaction to books is nothing new. Both states and churches have banned books from the earliest days of printing. What surprised Penguin and others in this case was that a religious leader in 1989 was not only seeking to ban the book but to have its author and publishers executed. The vehemence of the reaction was in part a product of domestic circumstances in Iran. The Ayatollah used the Rushdie issue to reinforce his authority at home. It was in part a product of global terrorism. In the wake of the Lockerbie air crash disaster, death threats emanating from the Middle East were taken very seriously. Another part of the problem lay in the development and organization of the publishing industry. Penguin were able to publish around the world and to orchestrate a publicity campaign which at first thrived on controversy.

This book was always destined for a world market and so comparative, international advice was vital as to its likely legal and social reception. The publishers were apparently warned, for example, that there would be a hostile reaction in India. For Britain, the legal advice would have been that there was no obstacle to publication since the blasphemy law seemed only to cover the Christian (perhaps more narrowly the Anglican) faith. Any ridicule of Islam would not therefore amount to a legal offence.

It was, however, easier to impose bans in other countries, and the controversy over the book in the UK threw into doubt the future of blasphemy law here. In the multi-cultural Britain of the late 1980s, it appeared manifestly discriminatory to have a law which prevented the distribution of a video deemed to be offensive to Christians but not a book that was offensive to Muslims. The government had failed to clear up the anomalies of the blasphemy law, perhaps feeling that it was unlikely to matter. Now it saw the costs of inaction. Half the country seemed to want the blasphemy law extended to protect Islam, half seemed to want the law abolished. Both solutions would have solved the discrimination problem, but with those behind crying 'Forward' and those behind crying 'Back', the government tried to stand its untenable ground, leaving the law where it was and issuing exhortations to its Muslim community entitled 'On Being British'.

One lesson that must be learned from the Rushdie affair is that the United Kingdom is in urgent need of consistent and defensible laws on free speech. Blasphemy should be abolished but incitement to racial *and* religious hatred ought to be offences throughout the United Kingdom. At present, incitement to racial hatred is not prohibited in Northern Ireland and incitement to religious hatred is not prohibited anywhere in Great Britain. My proposed reforms would fit more appropriately a changed society and our international law commitments. The restriction on free speech would be located at a non-discriminatory point and one which linked it with other limitations on free speech, where it was inflammatory to the point of endangering people's lives or safety. Moreover, we have seen that international law *requires* the UK to legislate along these lines under Article 20 of the International Covenant on Civil and Political Rights, which states that 'Any advocacy of national, racial or religious hatred that constitutes incitement to discrimination, hostility or violence shall be prohibited by law.'

Although none of these changes would have directly addressed Rushdie's book they might have prevented the sense of indignation felt by British Muslims at the way in which the law discriminated against them. It should be said that they also felt frustrated by the British media's lack of serious interest in their complaints about the book. These factors contributed to a climate in which opposition to *The Satanic Verses* took more and more dramatic forms, ultimately preparing the way for the Ayatollah's *fatwa*. While we might like other people to be more stoical about matter they find offensive, the reality is that the final claim of the playground chant, 'Sticks and stones may break my bones but words will never hurt me,' is just plain wrong. Words, or even images, do hurt people and they sometimes respond accordingly. British Muslim leaders felt that Rushdie, his publishers, the authorities and the media were not taking their sense of hurt seriously. All four were relying on a simplistic, sometimes selective, claim to free speech for the novelist. They seemed to be burying their heads in the sand of which the mythical city in Rushdie's book was made. In an interview in the Indian Press, published on 18 September 1988, Rushdie claimed that it 'would be absurd to think that a book can cause riots'. This statement was the best evidence that he was living in a dream world. While Rushdie had a platform for anything he wished to say about anything, his opponents in Britain, for example, could find few platforms from which to speak publicly against his book. Hence they felt they had to increase the stakes until they were listened to, through book-burning in Bradford. At that point, the white London literary élite began to pay attention. Their denunciations of the Muslims' freedom to express themselves through burning the book simply confirmed suspicions of hypocrisy in their defence of Rushdie's freedom of speech.

Another kind of perspective is necessary. There is nothing new in allegations of blasphemy. Jesus Christ was executed for alleged blasphemy. But there are many more modern examples from British history, some of which have uncanny parallels with Rushdie's case. In 1676 the deranged John Taylor was convicted of publishing a blasphemous libel in that he had called Jesus Christ a bastard and a whore-master and had declared that religion was a cheat. Lord Chief Justice Sir Matthew Hale said,

> That such kind of wicked and blasphemous words were not only an offence against God and religion but a crime against the laws, states, and government . . . and therefore punishable in this court, that to say religion is a cheat, is to dissolve all those obligations whereby civil societies are preserved; and Christianity being parcel of the laws of England, therefore to reproach the Christian religion is to speak in subversion of the law.

An Act passed in the reign of William III and only abolished in 1967 proclaimed that anyone who 'shall by writing, printing, or advised speaking assert that there are more gods than one, or shall deny the Christian religion to be true, or the Holy Scriptures of the Old and New testament to be of divine authority' shall be guilty of an offence. Meanwhile the common law offence of blasphemy continued to be invoked, as illustrated by the successful prosecution of a Cambridge don, Thomas Woolston, in 1729. He had written a series of pamphlets intended to show that the miracles of the New Testament had no place in historical reality but were allegorical representations of important religious truths. This was blasphemy, said the court, as was anything which struck at the root of Christianity. Critics of the law on blasphemy, together with critics of the Bishop of Durham, have pointed out that nowadays Woolston might have expected episcopal preferment.

In 1883, Lord Chief Justice Coleridge seemed to shift the emphasis from an offence against God to the control of immoderate language in declaring that 'if the decencies of controversy are observed, even the fundamentals of religion may be attacked without a person being guilty of blasphemous libel'. This would find an echo in some, although by no means all, of the Muslim critiques of Rushdie's novel.

Even this modified version of blasphemy law, in which it is allegedly the form rather than the content that is in issue, continues to attract criticism. It was well put by Chapman Cohen who wrote that 'Blasphemy laws are a heritage from a wicked and deplorable past. In their essence they belong to a period when laws were far more ferocious than they are today, and when it was held the duty of the State to enforce and openly coerce opinion.' This was written in 1922 in a pamphlet entitled 'Blasphemy – a Plea for Religious Equality', after the last prosecution for more than fifty years.

The next prosecution, a private one, was launched in 1977 by Mary Whitehouse against *Gay News* for printing a poem and illustration depicting Christ as a homosexual. The prosecution was successful at the trial (by a 10–2 majority verdict of the jury), in the Court of Appeal and in the House of Lords (by a majority of 3–2). The question for the Law Lords was whether the crime of blasphemous libel required an intention to produce shock and resentment among Christians or whether the crime could be committed by merely intending to publish a poem which had this effect even if the publisher did not intend so to upset others. If the latter interpretation of the law were chosen, the offence would be one of 'strict liability' and thus one could be guilty of it without meaning to offend, simply because people had in fact taken offence. If the former interpretation were chosen, then it might render nugatory the offence since it would be difficult to prove. The majority opted for the latter. Nobody now seems to think that this should remain the law (although that is not necessarily a criticism of the majority's interpretation of what the law *is*).

The House of Lords' judgments included at least two memorable judicial comments. Viscount Dilhorne declared, 'I am unable to reach the conclusion that the ingredients of the offence of publishing a blasphemous libel have changed since 1792. Indeed, it would, I think, be surprising if they had.' Although Prime Minister Harold Wilson once remarked that a week is a long time in politics, it seems that 197 years is not a long time in the law. Lord Scarman's contribution is justly more famous. He is widely regarded as the most liberal of British judges and usually escapes criticism from the left, who accuse judges of being conservative by instinct and training. Which way would he decide? For *Gay News*? No, he joined the majority:

> My Lords, I do not subscribe to the view that the common law offence of blasphemous libel serves no useful purpose in the modern law. On the contrary, I think there is a case for legislation extending it to protect the religious beliefs and feelings of non-Christians. The offence belongs to a group of criminal offences designed to safeguard the internal tranquillity of the kingdom. In an increasingly plural society such as that of modern Britain it is necessary not only to respect the differing religious beliefs, feelings and practices of all but also to protect them from scurrility, vilification, ridicule and contempt.

To complete this potted history, there were two further interesting developments in the intervening decade before we reach *The Satanic Verses*. First, the *Gay News* case went to Europe. It has by now become commonplace for disappointed litigants to say that they will take their case to Europe, although many are unsure about where in Europe they should go. Television news programmes, for example, invariably show pictures of the European Court of Justice (the EEC court) in Luxembourg, whereas human rights cases are actually taken to the European Court of Human Rights in Strasbourg. It is also commonplace to assume that the liberal European institutions will reverse the illiberal British law. Not so. The *Gay News* complaint was declared inadmissible ('manifestly ill-founded') on 7 May 1982.

The British government invoked three of the exceptions under Article 10 of the European Convention to the general principle of free speech; namely prevention of disorder, protection of morals and protection of the rights of others. The Commission rested on the last of these since it was a private prosecution: 'The Commission considers that the offence of blasphemous libel as it is construed under the applicable common law in fact has as its main purpose to protect the rights of citizens not to be offended in their religious feelings by publications.' Nor was the Commission impressed by the argument that the British law discriminates against non-Christians and could therefore be challenged under Article 14. Not so, according to the Commission: 'the applicants cannot complain of discrimination because the law of blasphemy protects only the Christian but no other religion. This distinction in fact relates to the object of legal protection, but not to the personal status of the offender.'

Perhaps nobody mentions this case because it was assumed that the law on blasphemy would not be needed again. After all, everything has been quiet, has it not, up to the Rushdie affair? No. Apart from various films which have been threatened with blasphemy prosecutions by campaigners, there was an interesting controversy worth recalling only a year or so before the Rushdie drama. Can you remember what was then described in letters to *The Times* as 'obscene' and 'most offensive' and the *Guardian* as 'outrageous . . . quite offensive . . . peculiarly insensitive . . . dangerous'? The offending item was a postmark authorized by the Post Office for franking the mail 'Jesus is alive'.

This gave rise to the glorious headline 'When franking incenses' under which Bernard Levin argued for a sense of proportion and tolerance. The Director of Development at the British Humanist Association had complained in his letter to the *Guardian* that 'those of us who believe that Jesus is dead – and have devoted some thought to the matter – do not wish to be told every day for six weeks that he isn't'. Mr Levin suggested that people who think like that should just throw away the envelopes, perhaps even mastering the skill of opening them with their eyes shut so as to avoid the message. Many Christians will agree. But some of them were not prepared to adopt the same approach to *Gay News*; that is to throw its blasphemous poem into the waste-paper bin or, better still, to refrain from buying it in the first place. Indeed, *Gay News* is less intrusive since it is not deposited through our letterboxes against our wills. On the other hand, no doubt those who prosecuted *Gay News* felt that it was wrong but that the Post Office is right, that they are justified in feeling offended whereas the anti-frankers are being hypersensitive. We have reached, in other words, a classic dilemma for a liberal, pluralistic democracy. To what extent should the law protect our beliefs from ridicule? How should we balance our commitment to our own faith with a respect for the consciences and sensitivities of those who have other faiths or no faith at all?

At a more dramatic, or rather violent, level, we have reached the same point with the reaction to Salman Rushdie's The Satanic Verses. What, if anything, should the government do?

The government is faced with the current widespread view that the law is unfair if indeed it only protects the Christian faith. As we shall see, even those who agree that the present law is unacceptable can proceed in diametrically opposed directions. The Law Commission majority thought that abolition was the right course. The minority felt that blasphemy should be replaced with a more coherent, enlarged offence. The government, through Home Secretary John Patten's letters to the Muslim community, seems to have rejected both conclusions. It seems to concede that the present offence is insupportable in principle but resigns itself to supporting it in the absence of any politically feasible alternative. This is not an unfamiliar position for government (see the whole history of Northern Ireland and successive governments' wariness of risking exacerbating the 'Troubles' through any initiative) but it has its own price (see the whole history of Northern Ireland . . .).

So long as the government believes there is no alternative, public dissatisfaction with the discriminatory nature of the law will remain. My own view, however, is that there is a way forward for the law. The principled argument for such a development would be the international legal norm mentioned above. The major attraction to me is that the focus of public debate would be shifted from the language of blasphemy to the language of protecting religious groups from hatred or fear. I realize, of course, that some people would not welcome such a shift. We will discuss its advantages and disadvantages anon. For now, let me just signpost this destination and return to the question of why it is we have not yet set out on that road.

The simple answer is that government and church reports have failed to get to grips with the tussle between freedom of speech and respect for others. The Law Commission majority, in particular, were also living in a dream world if they believed that any government was likely to abolish blasphemy without being seen to put something (almost) in its place. Meanwhile the churches seemed incapable of understanding the legal issues. Again, this needs to be put right. But first we need to trace the failures.

The competence of the Law Commission in this area is questionable. I am not here referring to the fact that two of the three majority Commissioners were recent appointments, one chosen for his expertise in conveyancing law, the other for her expertise in family law (much as that might be of interest) but rather to the Commissioners' own admission that 'In reviewing these arguments we are conscious that, as lawyers, we have no special qualifications for undertaking the task; a few of the commentators upon our working paper indeed queried our competence to consider a matter having theological and wide social implications.'

The Commission seemed to have no idea of the kinds of disturbances that might arise and indeed have arisen in the wake of publication of *The Satanic Verses*. The possibility of public disorder is either dismissed or described as 'remote'. This is not to condemn the Law Commissioners for lacking the gift of prophecy but rather to say that the whole document has to be read in the light of an assumption that is false.

The Law Commission rests its dismissal of the argument for the law to protect religious feelings on its denial that 'there is any real ground for maintaining that there is a difference between the reverence felt for God and other kinds of reverence, for example, for the Monarch or for parents.' This suggests that there is a long way to go before some people understand the nature of religious belief. Those who disagree with this premise may again find themselves reading a document based on an assumption they reject.

The lawyers having failed, enter the theologians. Although I have indicated that the government could be persuaded to move if a better case could be made than hitherto, the Bishop of London's Working Party was unable even to convince itself (in so far as one of its distinguished authors, Professor Keith Ward, soon announced that he had changed his mind), let alone anyone else. Yet this Report was forwarded by the Archbishop of Canterbury, Dr Runcie, to the Lord Chancellor. Dr Runcie had 'considered the Bishop's new Report with care' and said that he was 'happy to identify myself with its reasoning and conclusions'.

The Report recommends that parliament enact law to reflect the views of the minority who dissented from the 1985 Law Commission Report, that is, the existing common law offences should be abolished and replaced by a new statutory offence protecting all religions. This would penalize anyone who published grossly abusive or insulting material relating to a religion with the purpose of outraging religious feelings.

Surprisingly, the Bishop of London's group pays virtually no attention to the *Gay News* case itself. Consideration of the Law Lords' judgments would have put the problem in perspective, indicating the kind of publication in issue and the kind of problems which might arise. The Law Commission felt that this part of the law was unacceptably uncertain, that the Law Lords' conclusions on intention were unsatisfactory and that the limitation of the offence to the protection of the Christian religion was, in the circumstances now prevailing in England and Wales, unjustifiable. The Bishop of London's group endorsed all those sentiments. Two conclusions could have followed: abolish the offence without replacement, or abolish the offence and substitute a new offence which is in one sense narrower (requiring proof of a specific intention to outrage the feelings of others) but in another sense broader (applying to all religions). The Bishop's group took the latter path in the footsteps of the Law Commission minority.

This Report reaches the heart of our concerns when it criticizes the Law Commission for ignoring freedom of religion. The Bishop's group observed that the UN's Universal Declaration of Human Rights and the European Convention on Human Rights recognize not only freedom of expression, on which the Law Commission concentrated, but also freedom of religion as a fundamental human right. Some decisions under the European Convention were summarized in an appendix. Curiously, they omit the *Gay News* case which was itself taken to the European Commission. The conclusion there would have supported the Bishop's group since, as we have seen, the European Commission felt there was no doubt that *Gay News'* freedom of expression was limited by other people's freedom of religion and rejected the editor's claims as manifestly ill-founded. The group's rather patchy legal knowledge does not seem to have extended to this important decision. Elsewhere the Report fails to locate the blasphemy question accurately within the wider debate about when the law should intervene to protect groups from being offended – a debate which encompasses racism, pornography, the use or abuse of sex, violence and abusive language on television and much more besides.

The Report does however amount to a useful survey of some of the practical problems involved in reforming the law on blasphemy. If it is proposed to widen the protection afforded by the law beyond the Church of England, how is religion to be defined for these purposes? The group considered four possibilities: defining 'religion' in general terms; using the term without definition; listing the major religions with a power to add to the list by order; and defining religion by reference to religious groups having places of worship certified under the Places of Worship Registration Act 1855. They opted for the second course of action, or perhaps inaction, observing that the international documents already mentioned do not define the term and that the Indian Penal Code has operated for more than a century with an offence in general terms under which the deliberate wounding or outraging of the religious feelings of any person is prohibited. The group acknowledged that the adherents of some faiths which we generally regard as religious would not themselves accept that they are religious. The terms Hinduism and Buddhism, for example, are collective descriptions of beliefs, with at least one variety of Hinduism verging on the atheistic, but the group expected adherents of these beliefs to come within the protection of the proposed law. The beliefs the group envisages receiving the law's protection are perhaps indicated by another appendix which lists the 1980 statistics for religious adherents in the UK.

It is important to note these figures, since they reveal the multi-faith nature of British society and the rising significance of Muslims and other non-Christian faiths: Church of England 9,648,000; Catholic 3,182, 000; Methodist 651,139; United Reformed 222,049; Baptist 210,646; Jews 466,000; Muslims 830,000;. Hindus 380,000; Sikhs 210,000; Buddhists 121,000. This may well overestimate the number of *practising* members of the Christian churches and underestimate the number of British Muslims. The list certainly includes some people who do not want the protection of the law against free speech. As the Office of the Western Buddhist Order has observed,

> Buddhists do not want the protection of any such law. Moreover, we would prefer that the blasphemy laws be scrapped altogether and removed from the statute books, as we consider them to be an impediment to our freedom of expression as Buddhists. ... The highest tenets of the Buddhist religion are the Three Jewels – the Buddha, the Dharma (his teaching) and the Sangha (the community

of the Buddha's followers). The Buddha himself was quite explicit about how Buddhists should treat any indignity offered to the Three Jewels. In one of the oldest Buddhist scriptures, the Digha-Nikaya, the Buddha says: 'If outsiders speak in dispraise of me, or of the Dharma, or of the Sangha, you should not on that account either bear malice, or suffer heart-burning, or feel ill-will. If you, on that account, should be angry and hurt, that would stand in the way of your own self-conquest.'

The Church of England group, however, thought differently. It placed great store by the symbolic importance of the law:

It is often not so much what the law specifically says as the general underlying attitudes and values which it is held to express that are of importance for social well-being . . . Feelings for the sacred should not be undermined . . . We feel that the public debasement of Christian imagery, besides being deeply offensive to many Christians, may lead to a blindness to the things of the spirit and be seen as a corruption of the mind with regard to what we believe to be the most important features of human life.

The Report argued that the same respect for religious sensibilities should be extended to other beliefs, the proposed law thus forming

a cohesive and supportive element in the plural society of the country today . . . It is about the manner in which and the extent to which a person's deepest feelings about matters of the greatest concern are truly accepted within the community by being given the protection of the law.

This Report is therefore concerned with fundamental questions about law and morals and about the balance between tolerance and commitment in a pluralistic society. It rightly concludes by quoting the dissenting Law Commissioners who placed the onus on each of us to examine our own attitudes and practices. They urged us to recognize and implement 'the duty on all citizens, in our society of different races and of people of different faiths and of no faith, not purposely to insult or outrage the religious feelings of others'. This is, as I have stressed, not only a pious hope but also an international law requirement.

The UK's response to international law on this point, however, has been patchy. In England, but not in Northern Ireland, legislation prohibits race discrimination. In Northern Ireland, but not in England, legislation prohibits religious discrimination. In Northern Ireland, but not in England, there is a criminal offence of incitement to religious hatred. A British and Irish inter-church group has sensibly recommended extending the law so that it is consistent in all parts of the UK and conforms to our international law obligations. Race, sex and religious discrimination would be prohibited in all parts of the UK and incitement to racial and religious hatred would be criminal offences throughout the UK.

That is the good news for those who would like to see both consistency and fidelity to international law. The bad news is that the law in Northern Ireland against incitement to religious hatred does not work in practice. Some cynics would claim that it was designed not to work. In 1969 the Labour government in Westminster sent the troops into Northern Ireland only after the local Stormont Unionist government had agreed in principle to implement various civil liberties reforms. '[P]rotection against the incitement of hatred against any citizen on the grounds of religious belief' was one of the fields in which 'effective action' was 'fundamental to the creation of confidence'. Hence the Prevention of Incitement to Hatred Act (NI) 1970. In 1971 the Attorney-General for Northern Ireland explained the pitfalls in trying to prosecute under this provision, namely the necessity to prove that the words are likely to stir up 'hatred'; the necessity to prove the intent to do so; and the requirement that the hatred be directed towards a 'section of the public' (not an individual, not a church). The difficulties were evident when three people, including John McKeague, chairman of the Shankill Defence Association, were acquitted in December 1971 when charged under the act for publishing a book of 'Orange Loyalist Songs'. No prosecutions have been successful, few have even been pursued.

The 1965 Race Relations Act, which did not apply to Northern Ireland, seems to have had more success with its incitement to racial hatred provision (some twenty-four prosecutions and fifteen convictions in its eleven years). The 1976 Race Relations Act moved a new version of the offence into the public order legislation, removing the requirement to prove subjective intent. But when in 1981 the government appeared to do the same for Northern Ireland by moving its provision into a consolidatory public order law, it did not make the parallel change to remove the requirement to prove subjective intent.

Then in 1986 came a new Public Order Act for England which revamped the offence of incitement to racial hatred so that it now applies not only where there is intent to stir up hatred or arouse fear but also if, having regard to all the circumstances, hatred were likely to be stirred up or fear aroused. The Public Order (Northern Ireland) Order 1987 brought the Northern Ireland law on religious hatred into line.

A prosecution of Salman Rushdie in Northern Ireland under this provision would have raised interesting questions. For instance, it may be thought that the absence of the phrase 'religious belief' in the English law makes little difference. Given the broad interpretation of the word 'race' by the House of Lords in a case of discrimination, where Sikhs were deemed to be a race although they are in fact a religious group, is not the English provision already broad enough to protect Muslims from the stirring up of hatred or the arousal of fear? No, because the meaning of words like 'race' might be different in different legal contexts, so that there is more likely to be a strict interpretation in the context of a *criminal* offence, rather than the civil setting of a claim of discrimination. Even if Muslims were so protected, I should hasten to add, I do not believe that Rushdie could have been found guilty under such a law. I should also explain that, although for convenience's sake the offences are usually called incitement to racial or religious hatred, the full description reveals an extra element of fear. Their appearance under this umbrella demonstrates that they are seen as protecting the peace rather than religious sensitivities *per se*.

If an extended law along these lines would not have applied to Rushdie, what is the relevance of this debate to the furore over *The Satanic Verses*? It is important to appreciate that both the law and the *language* of the Rushdie debate have been vitiated by the concept of blasphemy. A shift in focus in the law might have diminished conflict and dissatisfaction. The frustration felt by those who were upset by Rushdie's book was certainly intensified by a sense of grievance about discriminatory law, witnessed by the way in which the issue of blasphemy became dominant. A law against incitement to religious hatred might well have contributed something positive in these areas.

Incitement to religious hatred can be distinguished from blasphemy in that it is more in keeping with the other acceptable restrictions on free speech and with that principle which John Stuart Mill and others have advocated as the crucial test of whether society is entitled to ban something: does it cause harm to others? Mill intended this as a necessary but not a sufficient condition for the law to intervene. Even if we count blasphemy as a harm for these purposes, it would only mean that society could invoke the law, not that it should. The moral high ground could be gained by other religious groups following the Buddhist lead and forsaking the legalistic terrain. This would be my own response. I do not accept that the law has no right to reflect the moral values of respecting the integrity of God or the prophets or of any living or dead person, but I doubt whether it is wise to stand on those rights. Others will disagree. In particular, some religious people might feel that to forego a law against blasphemy would amount to an acceptance of the majority Law Commissioners' crass view that reverence for God is just the same as other forms of respect. I suspect that this underlies the confusion of the Church of England's working party. They had some difficulty in justifying their privileged position under British law and were probably embarrassed by it, but they were trying to offer some way forward which would not be subject to the usual kind of cynical criticism by the secular media, that the bishops had lost their faith.

Incidentally, yet another irony in all this is that while the bishops fretted on this score the absolutist stance of many secular literary and media folk seemed to rest on some kind of quasi-religious respect for absolute natural rights, in contrast to their more usual utilitarianism. It is of course perfectly possible that a divine dispenser of natural rights would have picked the freedom of Salman Rushdie rather than respect for Himself or Herself as a fundamental duty, but it is difficult to believe that He or She would have defended to the point of immortality *only* Rushdie's freedom of expression and not, say, that of the book-burners.

Our present concern is that the *law* – as well as the bishops and the glitterati – has been exposed as hopelessly confused by the Rushdie affair. The lesson is that we should strive always to create a just and defensible system of law, rather than leaving anomalies like the present British blasphemy law. That law undoubtedly added to Muslim grievances and set the terms of the debate in the unhelpful language of blasphemy. Rushdie was seen by some British Muslims as guilty of what they felt ought to have been a crime. If, instead, the offence of blasphemy had been abandoned in favour of a prohibition on speech which advocated hatred of a religious group, the legal debate would have been on ground which could be defended as the proper boundary between the territory of free speech and that of respect for the equal dignity and security of all human beings. In my opinion, Rushdie would have been innocent. The law would then also have been innocent of the charge of partiality and thus innocent of aiding and abetting or inciting those who were offended by *The Satanic Verses*. Rushdie would presumably have agreed with the thrust of such a law and been perfectly willing to articulate, in court if need be, why his book could not be interpreted in good faith as guilty of any such charge as incitement to hatred.

Once the law is encouraged to think of protecting religious groups from hatred, or physical harm, should it go further and protect the group from other harms? In particular, should the law provide for group libel, on the analogy of an individual having his or her reputation lowered? Many problems immediately arise: what is a group for these purposes? Who could sue and collect damages if it is to be an action like individual libel? On what grounds is 'libel' to be elevated to a crime if the idea is, instead, that the state prosecutes on behalf of the group? Let us accept all these difficulties (which convince me, at least, that the cost of limiting free speech in this way is not too high) but focus instead on the strengths of this proposal.

Reflecting on how 'the group' may be defined is useful for a proper understanding of the Muslim reaction to Rushdie. It may be assumed that the relevant group for British law to consider would be British Muslims, but this is a group whose loyalties are divided between citizenship (British), ethnic background (perhaps Asian) and religious identity (Muslim). Muslims have argued that they see themselves as part of a worldwide community or *Ummah*. Hence the way in which the issue spread around the globe. It was not only the wonders of modern publishing but also the universality of the Islamic community which brought the matter to the attention of the Ayatollah. Only the most naïve observer could fail to note that the Ayatollah had additional, political motivations for issuing the *fatwa*. By taking such a dramatic step, he was able to reassert domestic control and make it difficult for other Muslims to oppose him, but he was at the same time responding to a genuine feeling that all Muslims had been diminished by *The Satanic Verses*.

There is indeed some support for a concept akin to group libel in traditional Muslim thought; more so, I would suggest, than there is for blasphemy. As the Koran puts it, 'O you of faith, let not one community laugh at another ... Nor defame nor be sarcastic to each other by offensive names.' There are plenty of other indications in the Koran that group libel will not be tolerated; for example: 'Those who love to see scandal propagated among the Believers will have a grievous penalty in this life and in the hereafter; God knows and you know not'; and again 'those who hurt through slander the believing men and women undeservedly, they bear the guilt of slander and manifest sin'.

Here is a more cogent reason for restricting freedom of speech than the blasphemy argument, although less persuasive than the incitement to hatred idea. It does not, needless to say, amount to a good reason for condemning Rushdie to death. Although our law does not recognize the concept of group libel, the matter deserves consideration. My own view is that we should not go so far in restricting free speech, at least until a reworking of our incitement to hatred laws has been tried. A half-way house between incitement to hatred and group libel is suggested by the recent legislation in New South Wales to prohibit racial vilification, the Anti-Discrimination (Racial Vilification) Amendment Act 1989. This makes it 'unlawful for a person, by a public act [defined as 'any form of communication to the public, including ... writing'], to indicate hatred towards, serious contempt for, or severe ridicule of, a person or group of persons on the ground of the race of the person or members of the group.'

A wide range of powers is given to a tribunal to order, for instance, apologies where appropriate. Prosecutions can only be brought with the consent of the Attorney General. There is a public interest defence for 'a public act, done reasonably and in good faith, for academic, artistic, scientific or research purposes or for other purposes in the public interest, including discussion or debate about and expositions of any act or matter'.

That defence should have protected Rushdie and no Attorney General would have been likely to have brought a prosecution. Moreover, this statute only protects members of *racial* groups. However, the legislation could very easily have extended to religious groups, and in the future statutes elsewhere might be enacted to move in this direction. The original impetus for this legislation had come from a private member's bill which would have made it unlawful (but not a criminal offence) for a person, by any public act, to vilify a minority group, defined to be constituted by race or the possession in common of linguistic, religious, social or cultural features.

Would this be a desirable development? The precedent for such a non-criminal restraint on free speech exists in the universal laws against individual libel. If we feel that free speech must take second place to an individual's reputation, so that large damages can be awarded and injunctions granted against repetition, why not do the same for groups? I have already described several difficulties in doing so. Not the least of them is how damages would be calculated – already a problem with individual libel law. In addition, many people regard the present law against libel of individuals as too great a restriction on free speech; extending its ambit therefore is likely to be unpopular. If we stop short of group libel and adopt the New South Wales option, however, other problems emerge. Before examining them, let us reflect on this innovative law's underlying spirit of respecting individuals' identities and sense of self-worth as being bound up in group membership.

Many law-makers in many countries, and certainly in the UK, do not understand what it means to think of oneself in any significant way as a member of a group. They find it difficult to conceive that those who feel less secure define themselves in this way. We ought at least to be open to the possibility that some version of a group libel action might be a useful addition to the legal armoury. My own view is that it would be fraught with difficulties, although it captures part of the Muslim anger with Rushdie and has, by virtue of the analogy with individual libel, a better fit with the other restrictions on free speech than has a blasphemy law. If we look again at the wording of the Australian development, the hatred provision is fair and proper but would be covered by my preferred Article 20 international norm. The other two elements 'serious contempt' and 'severe ridicule' – seem to me to be matters best left to privatized censors. Constant decision-making at what might seem to some to be a humdrum level will establish demarcation lines, whereas the full panoply of the law is likely to be utilized only rarely. Any judge and jury trying to define 'severe ridicule' will know it when they see it because they will be subjected to it by an incredulous media! The public interest defence will, in any event and quite rightly, safeguard most speech. I suspect, therefore, that such a law will amount to much ado about nothing. At the risk of seeming to protest too much, I must also stress once again that any half-competent lawyer would have no difficulty in ensuring that *The Satanic Verses* emerged unscathed from any such law. Rushdie would have been able to defend his book as a critique of all forms of fundamentalist intolerance rather than as denigrating Muslims.

I think that much of the fuss over Rushdie's book could have been avoided if we had had provisions in the law, other than blasphemy, that could have shaped public debate. It is astonishing, after all, how much emphasis there has been on the question of blasphemy. There is no concept equivalent to blasphemy in Islam. The nearest ideas are treason and apostasy – the forsaking of Islam for another belief or for unbelief – which many Muslim believed applied to Rushdie, and there is much debate in Islam on the appropriate response to such transgressions. The fact that these concepts were ignored in the rush to invoke the vocabulary of British law (albeit language which had almost fallen into desuetude) says something about the power of law to shape our arguments.

With better Acts of Parliament the debate could have been channelled into questions about whether Rushdie had advocated anything approaching hatred or had incited to hostility. This is the direction in which the law must go. 'No' would have been the clear answer in Rushdie's case. Instead the law seemed to encourage people to ask whether he had blasphemed, to which the answer might be 'yes' but to which the counter would be 'oh no, not against your religion, that doesn't count'. The desperate efforts of Muslim lawyers to challenge a magistrate's decision to throw out their attempted private prosecution of Rushdie showed how much the law meant to many of those British Muslims affronted by the book. They argued that the existing blasphemy laws could still catch Rushdie, either in so far as some of the book allegedly blasphemes against God or through judicial extension of the law to protect Islam. The clear statement of Lord Scarman in the *Gay News* judgment – that the law should be extended by Parliament – works against the Muslims on this point. Although he obviously felt that the law did not currently protect Islam, he thought that any change would be for Parliament to effect rather than the judges. No judge has subsequently seen fit to take another line on this question.

Let me then summarize this extended look at the law in relation to free speech issues thrown up by the Rushdie affair. My preference is for a law against incitement to hatred. I would not pursue the proposal of a group libel law at least until an incitement to hatred law had proved to be inadequate, if then. A group libel law is itself preferable to the present, or any reformed, blasphemy law. One way or another, it would have been desirable for the law to have pushed the terms of the debate away from blasphemy and to have given Rushdie's opponents a chance to air their real grievances in a dignified public forum, to have given them, perhaps their day in court. The law failed us, however, and it was the Ayatollah Khomeini who began to set the terms of the debate.

Sadly, British Muslims were not even given their day in the media. To what extent, for example, was serious Muslim dissatisfaction reported responsibly in the national press? How extensively did the press print examples of passages which Muslims claimed were offensive? Was anybody in the mainstream media really paying attention before the book-burnings? How many only took notice when the Ayatollah intervened? Did any national newspaper explain why the book-burnings happened in Bradford or whether book-burning had any particular meaning in Islamic culture? The Nazis did not burn books because nobody was paying attention to them. They burnt books because they were in power and intended to persecute dissenters. The Bradford Muslims, who were in any event perfectly entitled to burn their own copies, were not in anything like the same position. They were trying to get the indifferent media to listen.

At that point all components of the affair – particularly free speech – seemed to be in disarray. Would an apology from the author and publishers provide a solution? Rushdie's first reaction to the death sentence from the Ayatollah was to remain defiant. He reiterated the stand he had taken earlier. One of the inveterate contributors to the debate, Dr Hesham El-Essawy, chairman of the Islamic Society for Religious Tolerance in the UK, had reported Rushdie as telling him, on 30 January 1989, 'You want me to apologize. I will never apologize. I said what I said and will never stand down.' A fortnight later, Rushdie appeared to have second or third thoughts. On 15 February he offered a fulsome apology:

> As author of *The Satanic Verses* I recognize that Moslems in many parts of the world are genuinely distressed by the publication of my novel. I profoundly regret the distress that publication has occasioned to the sincere followers of Islam. Living as we do in a world of many faiths this experience has served to remind us that we must all be conscious of the sensibilities of others.

This seemed to be much more generous than the average apology for a libel. Mr El-Essawy thought so too, but the Ayatollah disagreed. The death threat remained in force and the Ayatollah appeared to take the view that there was now nothing Rushdie could do to expiate his sin. Four days after the apology came his answer: 'Even if Salman Rushdie repents and becomes the most pious man of time, it is incumbent on every Muslim to employ everything he has got, his life and his wealth, to send him to hell.' From my admittedly limited understanding of Islamic theology and jurisprudence, this is a highly questionable judgment. From an outsider's perspective, it has all the quality of lunacy.

By now attention was rightly turning to the effrontery of the Ayatollah's incitement to murder (our commitment to free speech rightly does not go so far as to permit what US constitutional law would call such 'fighting words') and diplomatic measures were taken to express disgust with this call to international terrorism. World writers united in statements invoking the guarantee of freedom of expression contained in the Universal Declaration of Human Rights (although, needless to say, they misleadingly omitted the qualifications therein). More helpfully, other Islamic foreign ministers repudiated the death threat. Their bans and boycotts of the publishers began to seem quite mild in comparison to the Ayatollah's opportunistic intervention, which was itself a cause of worry. By upping the stakes, the Ayatollah had left other censors in what seemed to be the middle ground.

Rushdie's apology was another cause of worry for some. What was he saying? Why did he regret the distress when he set out to provoke deep thought about fundamentalism? Wasn't distress the inevitable cost of his free speech and one which he should have accepted? What does it mean to say that we should all be conscious of the sensibilities of others? Isn't the point that everyone bar secular novelists was already conscious of those sensibilities, which is one of the reasons why they do not write such provocative books? And what does he mean by being 'conscious' of such sensibilities? Is he accepting that they are a cost of free speech which might on other occasions trump freedom of expression, or does he mean that they should just nag away at our conscience while we carry on distressing people?

Of course, Rushdie was apologizing under what amounted to duress. The Delphic utterance was no doubt meant to be capable of many interpretations. Since it was so imprecisely written some have even speculated that it was drafted for him by a committee of terrified non-Voltaires.

The next significant event was the American launch of the book. Many thousands of letters of protest were sent to the publishers; there were bomb threats and fears for the safety of staff in bookshops. The cost of free speech was running high, but hardly anybody seemed to be drawing up the balance sheet accurately. Two major issues still need to be addressed. Exactly what was it that British Muslims found so profoundly offensive? Second, exactly what is it which secures for authors a freedom nobody would expect in conversation?

On the first point, there were two reasons for Muslim outrage, only one of which has been much debated, the way in which *The Satanic Verses* seemed to insult, ridicule and vilify in a scurrilous manner the Prophet and the Islamic faith. The other reason Muslims were upset was because they felt that the book was attacking *them*. This was rarely articulated. The language of attack on Muslims, rather than on their faith, emerged from time to time even from religious figures. For this reason the churlish response of the British Council for Mosques to Rushdie's apology should be read carefully. Rushdie's statement was dismissed as not so much an apology as 'a further insult to the Muslim community as a whole'. While we might, and I do, disagree with their peremptory rejection of Rushdie's apology, we should take note of their terminology. It is the Muslim community which thinks it is being insulted. British Muslims felt demeaned by the book. They also felt that their fellow British citizens of other religious faiths and ethnic backgrounds would think the worse of them for subscribing to a religion which was depicted in such a way.

Nor is this a foolish fear. My impression is that the stock of British Muslims *has* diminished in the wake of the Rushdie affair although it is difficult to know what factors have contributed to this. A large part of the diminution has resulted from their failure to stand apart sufficiently explicitly from the Ayatollah's outrageous death threat (although, again, in the light of what happened to the Belgian mullah who took a brave stand, this is perhaps unsurprising). Another contributory factor has been the disorderly behaviour surrounding some protests. The book-burning has evidently (although to my mind unjustifiably) upset many non-Muslims. Then there has been the guilt by association (a fairly remote association in practice but not necessarily in outsiders' perception) with the Ayatollah. The book started all this and it *may* be that part of the damage to the external image of British Muslims can be attributed to it. I suspect that much more of the damage to the *self*-image can be laid at Rushdie's door. I do not think it is likely that many people would follow the line of thought which runs: if Muslims believe in something which is as ridiculous as Rushdie says, then we ought to think the less of them, for they must be idiots, but I can believe that a minority group might feel sufficiently paranoid in the aftermath of such a book to *imagine* that that is how others think.

Two further points about the way in which the problem might be seen by British Muslims as an attack on their group were well put in 1989 by the then Deputy Chairman of the Commission for Racial Equality, Professor Bhikhu Parekh, in a powerful article in the *Independent* soon after the *fatwa*. First, he detected an element of racism and anti-Muslim feeling in the reaction which lumped together all Muslims as book-burning, barbaric fundamentalists, so that British Muslims felt 'infantilised, ridiculed as illiterate peasants preferring the sleep of superstition to liberal light'. Second, the Muslim group can be seen as part of the Asian community which feels that 'those Asians who write, make films and television programmes or engage in instant punditry about them do not understand their innermost hopes and fears, and that they earn a handsome living and white acclaim by selling tired stereotypes and biased stories'.

So the new decade began with Rushdie still in hiding and the *fatwa* seeming to have survived the death of Ayatollah Khomeini. As the first anniversary approached, Rushdie attempted to break the stalemate. He published a long essay (the length strangely fascinating everyone, the article being everywhere described as a 7,000-word essay) in the *Independent on Sunday*, to which we now turn.

Only days after the text of this book was completed, Salman Rushdie wrote his own essay on his own saga. Not surprisingly, his article for the second issue of the *Independent on Sunday* achieved wide publicity. The paper also led with an interview, ran an editorial on the subject and reported the views of various members of the Great and Good on the desirability of a paperback edition. Michael Foot went so far as to describe Rushdie's contribution as the greatest polemical essay he had ever read. His other friends also expressed keen admiration. Two days later, a lecture written by Rushdie was delivered on his behalf by the playwright Harold Pinter and shown in full on BBC television. It too constituted a stout defence of the novelist's art, this time couched in less specific terms and written with more humour.

There was much speculation that something had gone wrong. Why was 'In Good Faith' not in the launch issue? Was there any haggling over the fee, reported to be in the region of £100,000 – quite a price for free speech? Or the copyright? Rushdie had become very particular about people quoting his free speech for free and had tried to prevent anyone learning of his 1989 poem through especially stringent use of copyright. I suspect that the *Independent* rightly judged that its first issue would sell anyway and shrewdly used Rushdie to keep publicity alive for the second issue. Anyway, those who admitted to not having read *The Satanic Verses* had for some time been saying, tongue in cheek, that they were waiting for the paperback. Now they could read Rushdie's summary of his own novel. Apart from that excellent précis, the essay was disappointing on several counts.

First, Rushdie said nothing about the people who had died, not even the Belgian mullah. Nor did he mention other innocents potentially affected by the deterioration in international relations, such as the hostages held in Beirut for far longer than Rushdie has been holed up in Britain. Second, he seemed hostile to other people's freedom of expression. For example, he criticized those who burnt books and, not surprisingly, those who called for his murder. He seemed particularly bitter about the failure to prosecute a Muslim for incitement to murder. Apart from expecting the law to restrain other people's speech, he used his own vitriolic prose as a weapon against anyone who dared question his wisdom. He was quite venomous about a playwright who had written a drama in support of him. Originally entitled *Who Killed Salman Rushdie?*, but subsequently amended to *Who Killed the Writer?*, the play was attacked by Rushdie as 'execrable'. We later learnt from the author, Brian Clark, that Rushdie and his agent intended to resist its performance: 'The irony of Mr Rushdie wishing to suppress a play because it offended him was so obvious that it became clear to me that he could not be thinking well.' A third deficiency was that Rushdie had nothing incisive to say about freedom of expression: 'What is freedom of expression? Without the freedom to offend, it ceases to exist.'

But what about the book-burners, even the offensive inciters? Rushdie consistently tries to deflect attention from the language he used, which was criticized as 'abusive and insulting'. He asks why he should not be able to challenge Islamic laws on such topics as women, punishment, homosexuality? He claims that it is the role of writers and intellectuals to ask awkward questions. Not all writers are intellectuals, or intellectuals writers, for that matter. Certainly, few intellectuals would have asked the questions he did in so provocative a way, nor, perhaps, could the Ayatollah have done anything about their impudence if they had been expressed in restrained language. One could perfectly well ask Rushdie's questions about non-Islamic countries in a way which would never inspire murder threats. I will. Why did the US Supreme Court recently support the constitutionality of the criminal punishment of homosexuals? Why has the Irish government done nothing to implement the ruling of the European Court of Human Rights against its laws, which also punish homosexual practice? There, nobody could be offended by the form of these questions. Rushdie could have asked them about Islamic systems in the same kind of language or about the American and Irish systems in more or less any language he chose. Where Rushdie ran into trouble was in asking questions in the *way* he did. He chooses not to address this central issue, nor to respond to the allegation of insulting Muslims.

Rushdie's arrogance is slightly less in evidence in his essay than in his usual public utterances but the accompanying interview reveals him still to be at times embarrassingly self-important. Indeed, the essay, inter-view and ICA lecture taken together suggest that Rushdie thinks art, particularly literature, and especially his own work, has taken over from such trivia as religion and politics as the guiding force for humanity. To the question 'Is nothing sacred?' he seems to be answering, 'Yes, the novel'. That, at least, is the thinly veiled subtext, however much that text itself may allow Rushdie to claim a more modest or realistic role. Notwithstanding his own clearly marked lack of sensitivity to political ramifications, the idea that the United King-dom might be ruled by Rushdie and/or his literary chums is clearly attractive to him in the wake of Havel's rise to political power: 'To have a serious writer like Václav Havel running a country, quite pos-sibly two serious writers if Vargas Llosa wins the election in Peru, is a sign that perhaps the world is a less hopeless place than I thought it was. It would be nice if it happened here.'

Sorry, Salman, it has happened here. Labour Ministers such as Richard Crossman, Barbara Castle, Tony Benn and Denis Healey must have spent much of their time in office writing their diaries, to judge by their massive memoirs. Michael Foot is a serious writer. Some would say that Ronald Reagan was a serious actor. Well, his wife Nancy would. There is no causal connection between being a good artist and a good politician. Havel is a good writer and a good politi-cian but it is absurd to suppose that all good writers would make good politicians.

Rushdie's essay has its strengths. In particular, he convincingly rejects the charge of apostasy, pointing out that since he never believed in Islam he could scarcely be regarded as an apostate. Curiously, the pluses and minuses of the essay seemed to get lost in the ensuing debate, which initially focused on the question of the publication of a paperback edition and was then hijacked by the Ayatollah's successor, Khameini, who issued a reminder that the *fatwa* was not negotiable, and a threat that Rushdie would indeed be killed.

The question of whether or not to issue a paperback is another case of much ado about nothing. The book was originally published in paperback in some foreign languages, including French and Spanish. The English language hardback is selling so well that a paperback is as yet unnecessary, even undesirable from a commercial point of view.

The possibility of withholding paperback publication is seen as an opportunity to resolve or compromise. Rushdie thinks that the long-term future of the book lies in paperback. Some opponents think that restraint, at least for a time, would be a wise peace offering. Of all the advice offered on this matter, the most intriguing (albeit misguided, in my opinion) came from James Kirkup, the author of the blasphemous poem which was the subject of Mary Whitehouse's wrath and prosecution in the *Gay News* case: 'No novel, however good, can justify the death of a single human being, and publication in Britain and the USA would be a useless provocation. Rushdie's novel is a tedious one, and not worthy of publication in the first place, so why bother re-issuing it in paperback?'

I suppose this drives home the truth that we all have our own limits of tolerance (a crucial issue to which we shall return).

As for the Ayatollah Mark Two, he continued to play on Western fears of Iranian terrorism. It has often been observed that the American, Russian, Israeli and British secret services have all targeted and assassinated people who are deemed to have spoken out of turn. The only new element in Iran's disgraceful behaviour over Rushdie is that its leaders have shrewdly judged that it serves their interests to announce their intentions in advance. If this is what is meant by open government, then it clearly has its attractions to some rulers. I have no hesitation in condemning the *fatwa* and in denouncing, as contrary to the spirit of Islam and the all-merciful reputation of Allah, the Ayatollah's insistence that repentance would be irrelevant. Nor do I have any hesitation in criticizing those (few) British Muslims who have lined up alongside the Ayatollahs and called for the death of Rushdie.

The *Independent on Sunday* deserves something close to the last word on the 'In Good Faith' essay, since it paid so much for it and also generously allowed dissenters to reply. It concluded that dialogue was the way forward but that British Muslims 'cannot reasonably hope to talk with Mr Rushdie, let alone win public support, while a gun is held to his head.' Since this newspaper has so far, in its short life, been preoccupied with Rushdie, we do not yet know whether it will adopt the same editorial line with Sinn Fein/IRA which holds a gun to the head of the British government and simultaneously hopes to talk. Before we address that issue, there is another way in which we can bridge the apparent gap between the Rushdie and Sinn Fein sagas. We need to consider the way in which writers have come to expect a sanctuary from violent reaction, which will in turn involve the question of whether the cost of free speech is the same for different modes of expression.

The final lesson of the Rushdie affair for our debate on free speech is that is it bound up in our understanding of the differences between various modes of discourse. The British comedian Jasper Carrott announced that Rushdie's next work was going to be a serious study of Buddhism entitled '*You're a Big Fat Bastard, Buddha*'. Similarly, the *Guardian* published an excellent cartoon which showed a Viking/ Penguin director saying, 'I don't know why he couldn't have come up with a scathingly satirical attack on the Quakers'. Now, we have already seen that Buddhists would not be particularly troubled by any such abuse and, similarly, we imagine that peace-loving Quakers are unlikely to punch Rushdie on the nose for any insults he might launch at their faith. But where I live, in Belfast, Rushdie might find himself exercising a little more self-restraint if he is ever in the happy position of being able to chat on the Shankill Road about Protestant fundamentalism or to discuss Catholic dogma on the Falls Road. No doubt he could produce some ingenious dream sequence which made fun of these religions but I doubt whether he would think it appropriate to try out his ideas by delivering his barbs in person. Yet he would, up till now, have presumably had no hesitation in writing the same material and publishing it as a novel.

Why is this, and are the conventions changing, or being changed, by Rushdie's experience? It seems that the customs and assumptions of literature are different from face-to-face discourse. Western authors have become increasingly accustomed to writing things they would not dare say in person. Literary kudos is more likely to be won by outraging than respecting. In Northern Ireland, it is my impression that people have developed sensitive antennae for discerning whether strangers are Catholic or Protestant, not because they want to offend them but because they want to *avoid* inadvertently offending them. At a simple level, let us consider the freedom to express the name of the place in which one is living. In a mixed group of Nationalists and Unionists, some people might compromise on the official term Northern Ireland.

In exclusively Nationalist circles, they would probably talk instead of the North of Ireland, while a group composed solely of Unionists might well use the term Ulster. Others will use their preferred term in 'mixed' company as a badge of honour or defiance, or innocently because of long usage in segregated life. Once anything more than terminology is under debate, people instinctively make all manner of accommodations and adjustments. In everyday life elsewhere, we all adjust our language – what we will say and what we will self-censor – according to circumstances. In the world of entertainment, one could argue forever about cause and effect with regard to self-imposed or externally directed censorship but whatever the reason some comedy acts are different on stage from performance in cabaret and different again in television appearances.

So, does anything go in fiction, and if so, why? The novel is a comparatively recent phenomenon of some three hundred years' vintage in the West and of this century only in the Muslim world. Part of the attraction of the novel is the possibility that underneath the veneer of fiction or even fantasy lies the truth waiting to be discovered. We want to know whether events depicted in novels, or something like them, really happened. On whom are the characters based? Some novelists refuse to participate in any such debates. Others let us know part of the story behind the story. When an academic character in a David Lodge novel finds that review copies of his first book have not been sent out, we wonder whether that happened to the academic novelist David Lodge. Yes, it did. When Rushdie writes a fantastic, in every sense, dream sequence, we want to know what he means about the real world, otherwise we would not bother to plough through a long and difficult book. In the Muslim world, however, as Professor Malise Ruthven, among others, has observed, the conventions are different: 'In Muslim countries private speech between individuals is much freer than that which is written.' Modern Western publishing has distributed a novel so widely around the world that it is ahead of its time in some places where much of the population is only semi-literate and only semi-acquainted with the idea of a novel.

This takes us back to the heart of what has been a long, sad but important story for free speech. Most discussion of free speech is conducted in simplistic terms. Speech is good, censorship is bad. If we get the right, liberal law, the free flow of ideas will make us better people. Every part of this summary is misleading. In particular, the law alone cannot solve the problems posed by free speech, nor can it always counter the Ayatollah-like threats to free speech. Free speech requires many other cultural achievements and values before it can thrive. Although liberty is often seen as the rival to equality, the two are mutually reinforcing in some respects. Without the confidence resulting from being accorded equal respect and dignity, a group will be reluctant to shrug off hurtful free speech. It makes no difference that such speech comes from someone who has some affinity with the group, and if members of the dominant group swarm to the defence of the speaker without understanding the concerns of the spoken-to, it reinforces the group's sense of alienation and fear.

All this has been prefigured in the chapter on the problems faced by ethnic minorities in the USA, while another lesson of the Rushdie saga has its parallel in my discussion of flag-burning. We can never be confident that our values are those of our neighbours. What seems ludicrous in Ireland may be acceptable in England and vice versa. What seems intolerable to five American Supreme Court justices can seem reasonable to four of their colleagues. If the British cannot understand the willingness of some Americans to curtail freedom of expression for the sake of a flag, why should Muslims around the world understand that the proper reaction to being teased and tormented in a novel is to display a traditional British stiff upper lip?

We must, in short, be vigilant not only against threats but also to build up support for free speech. The territory of freedom may be under attack from Ayatollahs. But like the imaginary city in *The Satanic Verses*, it is also built on shifting sands. It needs firmer foundations and we will have to dig deep to find them.

Part V   SINN FEIN

The other free speech issue which deserves careful consideration arises from the British Home Secretary's order to broadcasters in 1988 to desist from carrying direct speech by those representing groups sympathetic to terrorism. This must be understood in context and in the light of recent history. What then emerges is that government pressure has been continuous and too often covert.

The most amiable and unthreatening of journalists have fallen foul of earlier confrontations over television coverage of Northern Ireland. In 1959 the BBC caved in to pressure from the Prime Minister of the local Stormont government, Lord Brookeborough, and jettisoned without broadcasting half a dozen programmes by Alan Whicker after the first in the series had generated criticism. In 1971 the mild-mannered Bernard Falk was gaoled under the Criminal Law Act (Northern Ireland) 1967 for refusing to say whether Patrick Martin, who was being charged with membership of the IRA, was one of the two IRA members he had interviewed for the programme *Twenty-Four Hours*.

The BBC stood up to what was described by all sides as the most intense pressure from Reginald Maudling, the Home Secretary, and other ministers to stop a three-hour programme in 1972 called *The Question of Ulster: An Inquiry into the Future*. Again in 1979 it resisted calls from the Northern Ireland Secretary, Humphrey Atkins, to refrain from broadcasting an interview with a masked gunman from the INLA who had three months earlier assassinated Airey Neave. Then the Provisional IRA murdered Lord Louis Mountbatten and the BBC volunteered to the Home Secretary not to interview the IRA in the foreseeable future. Within months there was further trouble when a *Panorama* unit filmed an IRA roadblock. Although the film was not transmitted, knowledge of its existence was leaked to the press and led the Prime Minister to say in Parliament that it was 'time for the BBC to put its own house in order'. Taking the hint, the BBC sacked the editor of *Panorama*, Roger Bolton – although he was soon reinstated.

Most famously, the BBC Governors postponed the showing of the

1985 *Real Lives* documentary when the Home Secretary wrote urging them to do so in the wake of a speech by Mrs Thatcher in Washington lambasting those who gave terrorists the 'oxygen of publicity'. As Mrs Thatcher told *Newsnight* viewers on the day when the Governors acceded to Leon Brittan's request: 'Let me make it quite clear: yes, I do say things to the media, I do request them. But I am never going to put censorship on – we are not that kind of party.'

Then came the *Death on the Rock* documentary on the SAS shooting of three IRA members in Gibraltar and a subsequent inquiry headed by Lord Windlesham. When that thorough investigation cleared the journalists of malpractice, the government set about discrediting the credentials and independence of Lord Windlesham – a former Conservative minister. Soon after the Gibraltar inquest, the Home Secretary issued his order, revealing the government to be just the sort of party that would use legal powers to censor.

Or perhaps not. Mrs Thatcher might claim that the 1988 order is not quite censorship. In the words of Lord Donaldson, Master of the Rolls, in his 1989 Court of Appeal judgment declining to declare that the directives were unreasonable or otherwise susceptible to judicial review:

> Perhaps the most startling feature of the directives is how little they restrict the supply of the 'oxygen of publicity' to the organisations specified. They have no application in the circumstances mentioned in paragraph 3 (proceedings in the United Kingdom Parliament and elections) and, by allowing reported speech either verbatim or in paraphrase, in effect put those affected in no worse a position than they would be if they had access to newspaper publicity with a circulation equal to the listening and viewing audiences on the programmes concerned. Furthermore, on the applicants' own evidence, if the directives had been in force during the previous 12 months, the effect would have been minimal in terms of air time. Thus ITN say that 8 minutes 20 seconds (including repeats) out of 1200 hours, or 0.01%, of air time would have been affected. Furthermore it would not have been necessary to omit these items. They could have been recast into a form which complied with the directives.

Although one might prefer an alternative assessment of the Home Secretary's order – such as Lord Donaldson's description of the directives as 'half-baked' during counsels' arguments – this passage raised some important questions for the media. In the words of a student paraphrasing Lord Donaldson, we could say that what the directives achieve is to put something like the mark of Cain on the supporters of terrorism. While this seems insulting to the intelligence of the viewers, as if they could not discern the difference between constitutional politicians and those who endorse violent means, it does not necessarily prevent anyone from getting their message across to the viewers (unlike, for example, the complete ban on television appearances by Sinn Fein in the Republic of Ireland, which has been upheld by the Irish Supreme Court). But it does require us to decide whether there is anything in the argument that mere presence on the television screen (unless accompanied by some signal, like the use of subtitles or voice-overs) confers legitimacy or authority. This seems to be what irks the government. Is it a valid argument? The main lines of free speech debates were established long before the development of television. Does that medium's power justify occasionally reducing its impact to the level of other mass media, such as print journalism, by only carrying reported speech?

A second issue raised by Lord Donaldson's telling statistics is the self-censorship point or 'chill' factor. That is to say, since the limits of what is and is not permissible are unknown, do journalists play safe and self-censor rather than court the disapproval of the government or the courts? Given the importance and drama of events in Northern Ireland, why has there been so little coverage during the 1980s? It is partly explained by apathy or indifference (Northern Ireland's British problem?), but it is also partly caused by the media's fear of incurring the wrath of government – a fear generated by the incidents mentioned above, as well as many others chronicled by, for example, Professor Cathcart in his history of the BBC in Northern Ireland (*The Most Contrary Region*). The chill factor is often invoked by the media to explain their failure to work their way around government restrictions. It resembles doctors' claims that the law forces then into 'defensive medicine'. Perhaps the Home Secretary's tongue was in his cheek when he offered in Parliament as one justification for his 1988 order the fact that he was solving this problem for journalists:

From their point of view it is more clear and straightforward ... to operate under a notice of this sort, for which I take responsibility and which the House will debate, than to have to operate at their discretion, sometimes in difficult circumstances ... What it does is to state clearly and precisely an obligation with which the broadcasters have been wrestling, case by case and programme by programme for many years ... As they reflect on it they will see that this gives them a clearer and better way to proceed than they ever had.

If he had meant by 'difficult circumstances' to include behind-the-scenes government pressure (which he did not), then there might have been some merit in the government bringing its censorship into the open, but the ban is far from clear and the government has not yet shown how its order is preferable to the internal codes of practice worked out by the broadcasting authorities to deal with the coverage of those who support terrorism. Why, when the government had relied for so long on informal persuasion and the placing of sympathetic individuals in key positions (for example, through the Prime Minister's powers of patronage in appointing the BBC Governors), did the Home Secretary suddenly invoke legal powers?

Given the standard workings of government, civil servants were probably asked to produce a list of actions-that-could-be-taken-to-show-we-are-doing-something-about-terrorism. One of the options would have been to proscribe Sinn Fein. Another would have been to ban them from the airwaves. Each would have been accompanied by a list of advantages and disadvantages, probably all on one side of a sheet of paper. Addressing a possible ban, that sheet would probably have listed the following considerations:

For the ban
1 Would annoy the Sinn Fein leaders who thrive on publicity.
2 Would be warmly received by Unionists.
3 Would chill the media into further self-restraint.
4 Would imply that part of the problem in the past has been television coverage feeding terrorists the 'oxygen of publicity'.
5 One of the few measures to which the Irish government could not object since they have had a tougher ban on Sinn Fein for years.

Against the ban
1 International and internal condemnation of 'censorship'.
2 Could be counter-productive and increase support.

3 Could be defeated in court and will certainly be trailed through the courts all the way to Europe.
4 Could be counter-productive if Gerry Adams takes his seat as an MP to invoke parliamentary privilege (but highly unlikely the movement will let him).

Recommendation
1 Most attractive option.
2 Drafting crucial, preferably judge-proof but broad enough to leave TV authorities uncertain and on the defensive.

In my imaginary checklist, the cost of free speech is not mentioned, except in so far as condemnation from other countries, pressure groups or judges may ensue. This may be too cynical. Of course, in justifying or defending the ban, arguments about free speech would have to be deployed but they would not have been at the forefront of the ministerial debate. The Home Secretary would have called for an order to be drafted, consulted with the Secretary of State for Northern Ireland and put the recommendation to the Prime Minister. It would have appealed to her sense of dismay at the way in which television in effect encouraged terrorists to bomb their way on to the screens.

So the Home Secretary, Douglas Hurd, announced in the House of Commons on 19 October 1988 that he had just issued to the Chairman of the BBC and the Independent Broadcasting Authority a notice requiring them not to broadcast direct statements by representatives or supporters of proscribed organizations, together with representatives of Sinn Fein, Republican Sinn Fein and the Ulster Defence Association. The Home Secretary emphasized that the order followed 'very closely' similar provisions in the Republic of Ireland.

The Prime Minister explained that 'To beat off your enemy in a war you have to suspend some of your civil liberties for a time'. David Owen supported the ban in similar terms, 'restricting the civil rights of the few ... to try to protect the many'. Lord Mason, a former Labour Secretary of State for Northern Ireland, welcomed the ban although he did not think it went far enough in cutting off 'the oxygen supply of propaganda' from 'those terrorist groups who are bent on ... smashing our democratic institutions'. But another former Labour Secretary of State for Northern Ireland, Merlyn Rees, disagreed: 'It is a grave mistake and extremely foolish. The more you see of these people the better; when you try to hide them, they seem important.' Unionist MPs applauded the government but generally took the Mason line, thinking that the ban should have gone further. Northern Ireland's SDLP MPs and the British Labour Party took the Rees approach.

The broadcasting authorities seemed unsure what the order meant. They sought urgent clarification and received it from a Mr Scoble, an Under Secretary of State and Head of the Broadcasting Department at the Home Office, who met them on 20 October 1988 and explained the official interpretation of the ban. He soon confirmed in writing that in the Home Office's view voice-overs were legitimate, that works of fiction were not covered and that a representative of, say, Sinn Fein, could sometimes be regarded as outside the terms of the ban where he was acting in a personal capacity or as the representative of a council, depending on the context.

With little more than a whimper, the broadcasting authorities settled down to following the guidelines diligently. At first, they reported self-consciously that the coverage was compiled under the restrictions laid down by the Home Secretary, echoing the formula used in reporting under South African emergency law. Then they just stopped reporting what these people were saying – as happened in South Africa. The BBC and the IBA declined to take legal action to challenge the ban. That was left to individual journalists. When television did cover the views of representatives of Sinn Fein, sub-titles or voice-overs were employed. It was only after the Master of the Rolls had inquired why they did not dub in actors' voices that we began to see more creative efforts to get round the ban.

Both the Divisional Court and the Court of Appeal in England rejected challenges to the legality of the Home Secretary's order. At the time of writing, a separate case is awaited in Northern Ireland where there are additional distinct arguments against the ban. The major legal decision on the ban is expected from the English Law Lords when they hear the appeal from the Court of Appeal, a hearing which is scheduled for late 1990. Publication of this book, then, should roughly coincide with the second anniversary of the ban and the major court argument over the ban. In these circumstances, it seems appropriate to examine the legal issues in some detail. First, the actual text of the order needs to be understood:

1 I hereby require the IBA and the BBC to refrain from broadcasting any matter which consists of or includes:

any words spoken, whether in the course of an interview or discussion or otherwise, by a person who appears or is heard on the programme in which the matter is broadcast where:

(a) the person speaking the words represents or purports to represent an organisation specified in paragraph 2 below, or

(b) the words support or solicit or invite for such an organisation, other than any matter specified in paragraph 3 below.

2 The organisations referred to in paragraph 1 above are:

(a) any organisation which is for the time being a proscribed organisation for the purposes of the Prevention of Terrorism (Temporary Provisions) Act 1984, or the Northern Ireland (Emergency Provisions) Act 1978; and

(b) Sinn Fein, Republican Sinn Fein and the Ulster Defence Association.

3 The matter excluded from paragraph 1 above is in any words spoken:

(a) in the course of proceedings in Parliament, or

(b) by or in support of a candidate at a Parliamentary, European Parliamentary or local election pending that election.

Under British administrative law, such an order by a minister must not be illegal, irrational or procedurally improper. Another way of putting these three grounds of challenge is to say that the minister's action must not be *ultra vires*, unreasonable or contrary to natural justice. Several journalists, led alphabetically by Donald Brind, applied for judicial review of the Home Secretary's order. In essence, their claim was that the order was unlawful because it conflicted with the statutes which allegedly entitled the minister to intervene and that it was irrational because its 'solution' to the perceived problem was out of all proportion to the mischief being caused. Counsel for the journalists gave a couple of twists to the traditional way of arguing these cases. First, they claimed that the Home Secretary would be acting beyond his powers if he was contravening the European Convention on Human Rights. Second, they argued that there was a fourth ground of review, the concept of proportionality. In both respects, counsel were anticipating that they would ultimately have to fight this case before the European Court of Human Rights at Strasbourg. They wanted to use that court to force the British courts to address these extra points directly.

The Court of Appeal concluded that the journalists' claims were wrong, wrong and wrong again. They were not bound to take account of the European Convention, there was no separate heading of proportionality (even if there were the Home Secretary had not acted disproportionately) and neither had he acted unlawfully or irrationally. What should the House of Lords decide, how should it reach its decision and what implications does all this have for freedom of speech?

I have argued elsewhere – *Judging Judges* (1989) – that judicial decisions in such cases are influenced by three factors, only one of which is usually addressed openly. The first, and openly acknowledged, factor is the past law. The second is the judges' evaluation of the consequences of alternative decisions. The third is the judges' perception of their own role in our democracy. Within a few months of publication, it was gratifying to learn that judges as far away as Australia were already referring to this structure for analysis. Since this Brind case will surely attract worldwide attention, it is particularly important that the Law Lords similarly discuss all these diverse influences rather than pretend that the past law alone determines their decision. We deserve greater candour. Suppose they are prepared to argue about all these matters. What are the best arguments on each point?

The past law can be divided into the statutes specifically relating to broadcasting and the judicial decisions which have laid down the grounds of challenge for all governmental decisions. The order was issued under the authority of the Broadcasting Act 1981, in the case of the IBA, and under the Licence and Agreement, also of 1981, with respect to the BBC. The former reads: 'The Secretary of State may at any time by notice in writing require the Authority to refrain from broadcasting any matter or classes of matter specified in the notice; and it shall be the duty of the Authority to comply with the notice.' The BBC version was to all intents and purposes indistinguishable: 'The Secretary of State may from time to time require the Corporation to refrain at any specified time or at all times from sending any matter or matters of any class specified in such notice.'

Although these provisions seemed to give the Home Secretary *carte blanche*, other provisions appear to send conflicting signals. Thus another section of the 1981 Act imposes a duty to preserve due impartiality on matters of political controversy or relating to current public policy. Moreover, these authorizing statutes are always read subject to the proviso that Parliament could not have intended to give a minister the power to make an unreasonable decision. Furthermore, counsel for the journalists argued that the law expected the judges to conclude that Parliament could not have intended to allow the minister to reach decisions that were contrary to our international commitments under the European Convention, Article 10 of which guarantees freedom of speech. They were able to point to several examples of domestic judges drawing on the European Convention, most notably in the *Spycatcher* litigation. The Court of Appeal said that the *Spycatcher* case did not involve a statute so it was easier to read into the common law such a limitation, but where Parliament had spoken through a statute there was no legal precedent for invoking the Convention. As for the general principles, the old law seems content with three categories and, in any event, proportionality is covered by the term irrationality or unreasonableness.

My own view is that the Law Lords ought to conclude that the European Convention has been increasingly adopted by English judges for domestic consumption, to the point where one could say that the past law would expect them to ensure that the Home Secretary did not violate Article 10. If judges do not rely on the European Convention in this way, they will simply be delaying matters and wasting money because the European Court will overturn their decisions. On the other hand, the Court of Appeal stressed it is not the role of the judiciary to bring in by the back door what Parliament has deliberately kept out of the domestic legal system through its repeated refusal to incorporate the European Convention as a domestic Bill of Rights.

As for proportionality (the appropriateness of solutions to problems), this doctrine is indeed a useful way of characterizing one strand of the old law. So far as consequences are concerned, the Law Lords should accept that proportionality captures the essence of good administrative decisions, so that its introduction would be a beneficial development. Such a move would be well within the role of the judges to refine the common law. I do not think that it matters greatly whether proportionality is given a separate heading or not, although I would prefer not since it is difficult to separate such a claim from an irrationality test.

The weakness of the journalists' argument on proportionality was that counsel never seemed to be able to offer the lower courts a more concrete explanation than to say that it prohibited taking a sledgehammer to crack a nut. Before the Law Lords' hearing, they should scour the world for a more helpful exposition. In Canada, for example, the Supreme Court has developed a much more sophisticated test: first, is there a rational connection between the problem and the solution?; second, does the solution amount to the least interference possible to achieve the solution?; and third, will it work?

In one leading case, the Canadian government failed the first part of the test. The normal burden of proof in criminal cases is on the prosecution, but Canada had turned this about for someone found in possession of drugs, so that they had to prove that they were not trafficking. This was so even when the quantity of narcotics was minute. The Supreme Court held, controversially, that there was no reason to suppose that drugs users were drugs traffickers, so the government fell at the first hurdle of the proportionality test. If they had proceeded, the government might have failed the other parts of the test. Whether or not one approves of this result, overall this tripartite test clarifies what is meant by proportionality. Let us now apply the test to the Sinn Fein issues.

The first task is to clarify what problem the government thought they were resolving. An affidavit from Mr Scoble, the leading civil servant concerned, explained to the courts that the minister acted for four reasons:

The first was that offence had been caused to viewers and listeners by the appearance of the apologists for terrorism, particularly after a terrorist outrage. Secondly, such appearances had afforded terrorists undeserved publicity, which was contrary to the public interest. Thirdly, these appearances had tended to increase the standing of terrorist organizations and create the false impression that support for terrorism is itself a legitimate political opinion. Fourthly, the view was taken that broadcast statements were intended to have, and did in some cases have, the effect of intimidating some of those at whom they were directed.

There is at once a difficulty in that the much-vaunted restraint of the order, which allows the message to be given so long as it is not spoken directly by the representative of the listed organization, suggests that the measure is not going to solve any of these problems. Ironically, the government would have more chance of convincing us if it had taken more draconian steps, along the lines of the Irish Republic's complete ban on Sinn Fein representatives or supporters being televized at all. In one sense the Home Secretary retained a sense of proportion, trying to pass the second test by not doing more than was necessary, but he may have ended up by achieving nothing. Either there is a problem, in which case the 1988 order does not deal with it, or there is no significant problem, in which case any interference is unacceptable.

If the journalists present a coherent explanation of proportionality in the House of Lords, the government will thus have to produce a better justification of its measure. This raises the issue of modes of free speech again as there is the interesting possibility that what the government produces will take us forward to a world in which we no longer argue about the three justifications outlined above but discuss instead the *manner* in which different groups are allowed to participate in the democratic process, or argue that today's heresy will be tomorrow's orthodoxy, and so on.

For there is no ban. There is instead a restriction on the way in which those who support violence can get their message across. Unlike constitutional politicians, who eschew violence, those who support the gun are reduced to the same position they enjoy in print journalism: their message can be reported but they have forfeited the opportunity to put the point in their own voice. This is tantamount to a government health warning. Television is a beguiling modern medium, invented well after the basic lines of free speech arguments were established. If appearance on screen is not itself persuasive, why do companies pay so much for the advertising which sustains commercial television? Are we really as immune to the blandishments of Saatchi and Saatchi as we think? Those who pay for the advertising clearly think otherwise.

Appearance on television is a form of secular imprimatur, the label of legitimacy. The Irish government therefore withholds this imprimatur from Sinn Fein because Sinn Fein is pledged to undermine the Dublin government. The British government is taking a more restrained line, allowing the power of the medium to its sworn enemies and only interrupting their message by requiring it to be subtitled or spoken by actors. The government is, in short, putting the mark of Cain on Sinn Fein and, of course, on others who support violence. It is changing the relation between sound and vision on television in a way which parallels a device I used in an earlier chapter on incitement to racial hatred. Instead of spelling out a word, I asterisked it. This is an increasingly common tactic in American debates on this topic. Rather than spell out a racial epithet, the text is broken up even though everyone could supply the missing letter, as in 'J*p'. The purpose is to make readers aware of the hurt that such insults can cause by causing them to stop and think, where they would otherwise read on, perhaps oblivious to the insult. Similarly, the government here might say that if our most powerful medium, television, does not signal to viewers that Sinn Fein and company are different from other political parties, in that they wish to overthrow democracy through violence, then the government itself will have to asterisk each appearance. It is a constant reminder of their support of violence but one which still allows freedom of ideas – a moderate device to deal with immoderates in so far as it lets Sinn Fein get its message across.

To which one can reply: why not see, as we witness the second anniversary of the order, whether the public have absorbed the lesson to the point where we can try again to have business as usual? In the words of the Prime Minister, we were only meant to suspend our normal civil liberties for a while. The free speech debate has once again revealed a deeper problem: how should a democracy respond to anti-democratic enemies within the state? In bringing this issue to international notice, it has served us well. Now is the time to see whether our citizens and broadcasters have absorbed the lesson that we were becoming blasé about terrorist atrocities. The order was at best half-baked. The government should withdraw it before it gets defeated in the courts. Nevertheless the experience has been formative, causing us to sharpen our thoughts about the men of violence and about the political vacuum which allows them to survive.

Part VI   CONCLUSIONS

Disputes about free speech are almost always high constitutional moments or important episodes in our personal lives. They signal that something is wrong somewhere, either with the body politic or with ourselves. That something may have little to do with free speech. The Rushdie affair reveals much about the tensions and traumas of British Muslims and the complacent attitude of the media. The Sinn Fein saga shows how difficult it is to cope with a determined and skilled terrorist force while maintaining a commitment to the rule of law. Free speech is part of these stories but it should not dominate our responses to them so that we propose one placebo for a symptom rather than a treatment for the cause of the illness and preventive measures to stop other outbreaks.

In so far as the reason for a free speech dilemma really is a threat to free speech rather than an indication of breakdown elsewhere in our political or cultural life, then the thrust of this book has been that the threats of the future are more likely to be subtle and privatized, rather than obvious and state-sponsored. Eastern European (and, dare I add, South African) regimes of censorship seem to be crashing as I write. I am not so naïve as to suppose that the statute books around the globe will now always favour free speech, still less that practice will reflect legal theory. Moreover, I have already indicated that such a development would be positively unwelcome, given that other values must sometimes trump free speech. Nor do I think that the more insidious forms of control are only a recent phenomenon.

However, in the past such subtle pressures were less worrying than the major repression. It would have been heaven for dissident writers to be preoccupied only with incurring the displeasure of employers at a time when the full force of the criminal law was being deployed to silence them. Now that the state is giving up the unequal struggle against the power of ideas, we have to think seriously about the legitimacy and limits of privatized pressures.

Once we have established our views on the proper response to such pressure, there remains another task that has been too often undervalued in previous discussions of free speech, namely building up support for the free flow and critical reception of ideas. Pope Paul VI once said that peace is more than the absence of war. Similarly, free speech is more than the absence of censorship. Peace can only be built on structures of justice, while free speech can only be supported by a continuous commitment to education. At the most basic level, I would like to see an interpretation of the right to freedom of speech which emphasized the importance of universal literacy. Command of the written language is not high in many Muslim countries, for example, and command of spoken, let alone written, English is not high among some immigrant communities in the United Kingdom. More ambitiously, a commitment to achieving standards of primary and secondary education across a wider field than literacy is the next essential. In particular, the ability to analyse information and opinion critically is one of the most important corollaries to a free marketplace in speech.

In other words, the battle for free speech in the 1990s is not so much about freeing the Salman Rushdies of this world, much though I wish that to happen, as empowering the imaginations of those who have not heard of Rushdie or who do not have the skills to read his writing, the understanding of the genre necessary to appreciate the book (a group which would include most of the world) or the time, energy, stamina and powers of concentration to get through it.

This aspect of the fight for free speech is not just about the mechanical skills of reading and writing. There are also cultural barriers to be considered. After due reflection some will want to maintain such restrictions, others will seek to bring the walls tumbling down. For example, one frustration for many journalists and sociologists trying to understand the British Muslim reaction to Rushdie has been the feeling that some young Muslims regard it as beyond limits to question the wisdom of their elders. This was in the past a phenomenon familiar to many other groups, such as Catholics, and some Catholic clergy still find it difficult to come to terms with a more questioning laity. Ironically, it is part of the claim of this book that it is the liberal intellectual elite which now finds heresy outrageous. It may be that Catholics felt less inclined to question when they regarded themselves as under threat in a hostile British environment, that Muslims find solidarity preferable to critical inquiry because they are still subject to discrimination, and that liberals have become less liberal as they have experienced a decline in confidence after many years in the British political wilderness. This would explain why I have experienced a culture shock in moving to Northern Ireland where the mildest public criticism of the Catholic Church's opposition to integrated schooling is regarded by some clergy as a qualification for being burnt at the stake and many priests and parishioners who agree with me are only willing to do so in hushed tones, lest Father find out. In a society which treated Catholics badly for fifty years, the Catholic schools were a haven of self-determination. Hence even to suggest that the resulting self-induced segregation is also part of the problem, or to suggest an experimental openness to a potential solution, is seen as dangerous heresy.

We will not have the right pre-conditions for free speech within such minority groups unless and until such groups have the self-confidence which comes from being respected and accepted. That is why the Rushdie affair strikes at the heart of the issue in such a paradoxical way. *The Satanic Verses* has been seen by Muslims as an attack on them at a time when they are still a vulnerable group in British society. It is ludicrous for British law to protect a privileged group like Anglicans from such scurrilous attacks. Precisely because they are a privileged group, Anglicans are in a position to treat blasphemy with disdain or indifference, as saying more about the hang-ups or commercial aspirations of the film producers, poets or novelists who produce the blasphemy than about the faith they seek to denigrate. If there is an argument at all for defending the present law against blasphemy I would couch it in terms of life having passed Anglicans by to the point where their beliefs are no longer dominant but are regarded as quaint in a secular society. The writing was on the wall, on this view, when the old joke about the Church of England being the Conservative Party at prayer was adapted, given the political naivety of some prelates, to the Social Democratic Party at prayer. Given the speed at which support for the SDP has collapsed, and given the middle ground's love of relabelling itself, events would then indicate that the Church of England could now fit into smaller pews and should be retitled the Side-Chapel of England.

If this is a correct analysis, if Christianity has become a minority way of life, then perhaps Anglicans and others might mount an argument for the law's indulgence based on weakness rather than historical strength. I find racist hate speech obnoxious in all its manifestations, and can see the egalitarian reasons for prohibiting all of it, but in practice there is little need in the real world of Britain today to protect the sensitivities of whites. Hence, those of us who regard free speech as important might well argue that restrictions should always be scrutinized rigorously and cannot be as necessary to protect a dominant group as they might be to defend a beleaguered minority. Thus, in religious terms, I would prefer to see British and Israeli law protecting Muslims, with Iran protecting Christians and Jews. That will be the day!

But to return to cultural restraints on free speech, do we want to break the taboo of criticizing elders or religious orthodoxy? My own view is that we do, but, as with the argument throughout this book, it depends on taking people with us on a crusade for a responsible attitude to free speech. The cultural inhibition of such criticism is partly caused by the lack of confidence one expects in a minority, the ghetto complex we have just explored, but it is partly a function of misunderstanding the nature and motivation of criticism. If criticism is perceived as disrespectful and hurtful, then no wonder it is viewed with suspicion. This is not to justify those who use such suspicion as an excuse for a violent reaction, but it is to argue for the need to *explain* the function of critical literature rather than simply to start selling it to an unready, sensitive minority British Muslim readership.

Glasnost, or openness to criticism, and perestroika, restructuring, might seem appropriate rallying cries with which to end a book on free speech. Toleration, in contrast, is so unlikely to feature as a catch-phrase that its Russian equivalent is as yet little known to the outside world. Toleration is seen as an old-fashioned virtue, if it is seen as a virtue at all.

Is toleration understood, even by those who profess it? I hope this book has caused one or two of my fellow liberals to reassess our too easy recourse to some standard free speech rhetoric. As a parting shot, let us consider what we mean by toleration. Joseph Raz has defined toleration as

> the curbing of an activity likely to be unwelcome to its recipient or of an inclination to act which is in itself morally valuable and which is based on a dislike or an antagonism of that person or of a feature of his life, reflecting a judgment that these represent limitations or deficiencies in him, in order to let that person have his way or in order for him to gain or keep some advantage.

Suppose, as seems to be the case, that Rushdie is antagonistic to the intolerance of fundamentalist Islam. Rushdie might well feel that it is morally valuable for him to expose Islam to ridicule so as to make fundamentalists think seriously about their faiths. He may even dislike particular features of Islamic life, such as the relationship between men and women. If Rushdie is to be tolerant in Raz's sense, however, none of this necessarily justifies writing a pugnacious work of fiction. On the contrary, we are setting up precisely the conditions where tolerance could come into play and where it might suggest restraint. It does not follow that toleration will, or should, prevail over other values in any particular case, but it does suggest that *contemplating* self-restraint is the hallmark of a tolerant person. There is no virtue, so to speak, if one is not tempted to be intolerant.

Now, a corollary of all this is that the mere assertion of a right to free speech is never enough to satisfy those of us who believe it is part of the human condition to strive always for higher moral ground, for there is always the possibility of over-trumping the rights card by playing the ace of toleration (or other cards, such as respect for the equal dignity of women or ethnic minorities or for privacy). Where Rushdie has antagonized many is in seeming to have ignored the possibility of tolerating the evils of fundamentalism. Yet we know also that there comes a point when it becomes intolerable to tolerate the intolerant. How do we know whether that point has been reached?

This book has sought to give some indications. The first piece of advice is to be vigilant, as John Philpot Curran recommended two hundred years ago. The second is to note that we are all censors now. The privatization of censorship has placed us all in positions of responsibility as to how we use our speech. The third is to appreciate that there are always costs to free speech and that the cost must be high before we can contemplate preferring another value.

However, none of this solves the particular problem of when to tolerate and when to use free speech to attack. We must ask deeper questions, such as why toleration, or for that matter free speech, is valuable. The answer is probably that we value autonomy, the freedom to think and act on one's own reasoning, to do one's own thing. This does not mean simply living and letting live as though we were isolated individuals. Respect for other people's autonomy some-times means leaving them alone, but often it requires governments, at least, to intervene in our lives, so as to provide compulsory primary and secondary education, for example. Intervention is necessary to develop our critical faculties, otherwise we cannot be said to be genuinely 'choosing' one way of life rather than another. Moreover, we must have some alternatives from which to select, which may again demand intervention through such mechanisms as social security. Autonomy is not an all or nothing, one-off, feature of our lives. We have autonomy over time. At some times free speakers can help us become more autonomous by enhancing our self-awareness, by showing us that atheism, Islam, Judaism, Christianity and other approaches are all possible. At other times, when we are weak, autonomy is better served by building up self-confidence than by undermining self-respect. Within all of this, of course, one might legitimately ask whether autonomy is an end-in-itself or a means to some other end. Is there a value in choosing, albeit 'wrongly', or is the point rather that we are more often likely to know what is good for ourselves?

The upshot of all this is that there never can be one easy answer to all free speech questions. Indeed, it is the easy answer which is almost certainly wrong, if only because it suggests that the full range of considerations have not been examined. The Ayatollah and the IRA, the inventor of Mrs Torture together with the real Mrs Thatcher, all have a reputation for regarding those who are not with them one hundred per cent as being against them. Those who recognize the costs of free speech, however, are inclined to value the chance to argue the pros and cons, to take criticisms and fallibility seriously. The danger is that such people will seem less committed to whatever emerges from that careful thought process.

Two years on from the Home Secretary's order banning direct speech by groups sympathetic to terrorism, I think that the government should make good its implied pledge that civil liberties would be suspended only *for a time*. The restrictions have served the purpose of making journalists confront the moral dilemmas inherent in reporting the apologists of terrorism. Although I think they were already engaged in such self-examination, some good may have come from being forced to reconsider the rights and wrongs of free speech. Two years on from the publication of Rushdie's book, the *fatwa* has certainly caused many people to stop and think about the power of the word. International and national pressure must be brought to bear more effectively to rescind the instructions to death squads to seek out Rushdie. Writers and their critics must then show that they have thought about their mutual responsibilities. As Julian Barnes observed in *Flaubert's Parrot*: 'Some Italian once wrote that the critic secretly wants to kill the writer. Is that true? Up to a point. We all hate golden eggs. Bloody golden eggs again, you can hear the critics mutter as a good novelist produces yet another novel; haven't we had enough omelettes this year?'

In this last chapter, I wish to reflect on the issues raised throughout the book and to reiterate the point that free speech crises themselves reflect deeper problems within societies.

Voltaire

Voltaire's supposed saying has led us astray. This is not to deny that there *are* people who spend their lives standing up for those whose views they dislike. When a Belfast solicitor, Paddy McGrory, was accused by a British newspaper of being sympathetic to the Republican terrorists for whom he acted, he received death threats. Given the murder of a fellow local solicitor, Pat Finucane, after similar accusations, these were not to be taken lightly. Mr McGrory did not go into hiding. He carried on his work and took action to clear his name. When he won substantial damages in the subsequent libel case, one of the first people to congratulate him was a suspected Loyalist terrorist. Mr McGrory had defended that man, just as he had represented alleged Republican terrorists. Nobody could approve of what *both* Loyalist and Republican terrorists say and do. As the election performance of Sinn Fein demonstrates, few approve of any kind of terrorism. Lawyers who disapprove of what their clients have said or done nevertheless are prepared to defend to the death their right to representation in a fair trial.

And there are even better examples of people who have died more specifically for free speech, most notably the Belgian mullah, Abdullah Al-Ahdal, who defended Rushdie. But everyday support for free speech is much less dramatic than the kamikaze image conjured up by those who invoke the magic Voltaire saying. We need to move beyond the glib catch-phrase in our support of free speech.

Privatization of censorship

Alternatively, if we must pin our hopes on a quotation, then it should be Curran's aphorism about the need for eternal vigilance. In which case, we must know where to look, which is not simply towards government. Information is power. All sorts of groups who control the flow of information have an effect on our ability to receive and impart knowledge. For example, journalists are far more affected in their coverage of Northern Ireland by the need to keep on good terms with their sources, principally the police, than they are by the government's 'ban'. Those who write unfavourable reports may find doors closed, telephones hung up, and no story next time round. For too long we have thought about free speech in terms of what we can say about ministers who ban forms of free expression. This happens and must be countered effectively. But we must also address the concentration of censorial power in private hands, our hands. We must also move beyond the legal right to free speech and begin debating the rights and wrongs of exercising this right in particular ways at particular times. Publishers, for example, are continuously engaged in such discussions. Would Viking Penguin have done *nothing* differently if they had had the gift of prophecy? It was, until the *fatwa*, publishers' nature to court controversy. There is nothing better than a ban or a fuss for sales – look at the commercial success of an appalling book, *Spycatcher*. No doubt many publishers will be more likely to tone down, rather than play up, controversy if it may lead to another *fatwa*. So we are all censors now, ayatollahs, terrorists, publishers, authors.

Costs

Moreover, what is, in this broad sense, censorship is sometimes justified. The next lesson for free speech is to accept that it is costly. We get nowhere by pretending that there are no other important, conflicting values. Rushdie was quite right to eschew any line of defence which even hinted at the claim 'Oh well, it was only a novel, it wasn't serious'. Novels can be serious. Words can be powerful. The playground chant about words or names, unlike sticks and stones, never hurting us is simply wrong. Incidentally, have you noticed that children only resort to this mantra when they *have* been temporarily wounded by some name-calling but cannot think of any like response?

Privacy

The value which most clearly seems at odds with free speech is privacy. I am less worried about the law, much as I think that the law in this area is in disarray. I am more concerned that we have not properly thought through the conflict at the moral level. Like the judge in the 'lesbian pillow talk' case, I tend to think of us as having spheres or zones of privacy, one of which protects our intimate relationships. On the other hand, like American law, I would suggest that those who voluntarily (and sometimes, sadly, involuntarily) enter the public arena forfeit their right to privacy where their behaviour reflects on their trustworthiness or other capabilities for public office. British newspapers are facing the prospect of law reform designed to strengthen the right to privacy in the face of their investigative reporting. They have responded by developing their own code of practice and system of ombudsmen. Whether or not this heads off the pressure for a more restrictive legal framework is less important than the fact that public concern has made the press face up to the conflict between free speech and privacy. It is of particular interest that the irresponsible exercise of the right to free speech in the recent past is in danger of narrowing the scope of free speech in the future. Let me make explicit what has, I hope, been implicit in many chapters: it is myopic to defend free speech solely by reference to legal rights. This misses the point that legal rights are dynamic, in flux, and that the condition upon which the legal system has given us freedom is that we exercise it with a sense of proportion.

Pornography

If any particular example, or class, of pornography could be demonstrated to be the cause, rather than the occasion, of violent and/or sexual assault, that would be a clear reason for restricting, or even prohibiting, access to it. In practice, such proof is difficult to gather and will come, if at all, too late. So we are often faced with questions about the burden of proof – should we err on the side of speech or safety? Moreover, there is a considerable body of opinion that claims that pornography is a symptom rather than a cause. Where the pornography does not lead to specific attacks but nevertheless degrades women there is even more reluctance to take action. In these circumstances, censorship is a second best option, although I would not rule it out as a temporary measure. The best solution, however, is clearly to facilitate opposing speech, which reinforces the equal dignity of women and which pities the inadequacies of those who are involved in the pornography industry, and above all to develop a society in which women are accorded that equal respect.

Again, I hope that on reflection readers will see latent in the chapter on pornography an argument which is made explicit in the Rushdie section, that the call of censorship is often from a group which sees itself as otherwise threatened or under-valued in society. Rather than concentrate exclusively on the free speech question, it is necessary to work for the right social conditions to allow the worried group, be they Muslims or women, to feel secure. The literary or political or media establishments are full of non-Muslim males, like myself, who can easily ignore any offence that may be caused by insults to another religion or the other sex. Instead of telling British Muslims or British women to pull themselves together and develop a stiff upper lip like a good chap, and instead of alternatively giving in to all demands for censorship, we must work for a society in which other groups have the same self-confidence, which can only come through being genuinely respected as equals. A good test of the fact that different groups are threatened by what seem to others to constitute the most natural surroundings or comments is to think how men and women, or say whites and Blacks, react upon entering a large gathering, such as a busy pub. Members of the dominant group, white males, are unlikely to be bothered by who else is there. A Black woman, however, is likely to look round to see whether other women or Blacks are there in any numbers. If they are not, she is likely to feel slightly uneasy, especially if comments are made which in other circumstances she might be able to ignore with equanimity. If we really value free speech, we must work for the right pre-conditions in which it, and all of us, can flourish.

Incitement to racial hatred

The arguments of the preceding paragraph were more explicit in the chapter on incitement to racial hatred. The reason is that such incitement is more clearly motivated by hate and has fewer, if any, beneficial aspects, whereas pornography is usually motivated by money and has some, albeit often spurious, claims to be valuable. I concluded here that

the United Kingdom and other countries should honour their international law commitments to prohibit such incitement. In the light of
later chapters, it should be clear that such laws would have had a role to
play in reorientating the terms of the debate about *The Satanic Verses*,
although there can be no question but that Rushdie would have been
innocent of any charges of incitement to hatred. Again, the law is not an
end in itself and cannot be judged by the number of successful prosecutions. It is symbolic of our limits of tolerating the intolerant and of the
point at which, but not before, it is necessary to sacrifice free speech.

Flag-burning

I concluded here that the decriminalization of such expressive conduct
by the US Supreme Court majority was desirable but that it highlighted
a paradox which resurfaces in many forms throughout free speech
arguments. Should conservatives advocate a free market in free speech
or a concern for traditional values? The flag-burning issue is merely the
most dramatic reflection of this tussle. There are few more poignant or
eloquent defences of the primacy of free speech in such conflicts than the
judgment of Justice Brennan.

Official secrets

Like the media, I am deeply suspicious of all governmental claims of
official secrecy. Once again, the government has done itself no good by
trying to rely on what it sees as its strict legal rights rather than
reflecting on why free speech issues arise in this area and then attacking
the root causes of the problems. Unlike the media rhetoric, although I
suspect like media practice, I do however accept that some claims of
official secrecy would be legitimate. The government has compounded
its short-sightedness by adopting a policy of 'if it moves, ban it' rather
than sometimes playing down the significance of publications. I can
understand the principle of a worldwide legal battle against *Spycatcher*
but the effect was to publicize an otherwise undistinguished and
implausible book. The latest official secrets legislation has one redeem-
ing feature, that it recognizes different levels of official information.
Unfortunately, virtually everything is then placed under the category
which will be kept secret. The better way forward is for governments to

admit the public interest in freedom of information, to make a wider circle of official information available, and then to defend with more credibility a more closely targeted range of genuine secrets.

Arguments

While the press can be relied upon to police the government on official secrets, they cannot be relied upon to police themselves. In particular, there is too much reliance on weak arguments for free speech, which again undermine the good arguments. What we do need to do is to rediscover, in public debate, a passion for the core of free speech. At present, however, the assumption is often that you can only be committed to free speech if you are prepared to spend your time arguing for Nazis and pornographers. On the contrary, it is legitimate to question the parameters of free speech, to hone the arguments for that expression and then to defend that narrower ground as vigorously, and with more plausibility, than the absolutist rhetoric so often employed today. I hope this book encourages such a reassessment.

Salman Rushdie

The law on blasphemy, the timing of the paperback edition and the appalling reaction of the Ayatollah Khomeini should not dominate debate on the Rushdie saga. For the record, I should clarify that I would abolish the law on blasphemy and that I would publish the paperback when it was commercially right to do so. While the English language hardback is selling well, there is little point. When will we see a paperback of Stephen Hawking's scientific blockbuster? Certainly not while it remains on the bestseller list as a hardback.

Moreover, the Ayatollah's death threat is intolerable, as is support for it. Everything must be done to protect Rushdie and his publishers, as it must for the less famous in Northern Ireland and elsewhere who have long been under death threats for speaking their mind.

Rushdie is already showing signs of emerging as not only a sadder but also a wiser man. The arrogance of the free speaking secularocracy has been dented. Again, the message of the free speech *cause célèbre* has been that the crisis reflects a deeper social problem, in this case the way in which British Muslims have felt unwelcome in our society. That does not excuse the Ayatollah or other politicians jumping on the band-wagon, but it does raise question marks about the wisdom of a British author using Islam as the faith on which to hang the charge of fundamentalism. Of course, Rushdie is right to say that the worldwide strength of Islam is enormous and ought to be able to withstand his critique. Of course, he was more knowledgeable about Islam so that a comparable work picking on Catholics or Protestants would have required more research. And the other theme of the novel, displacement, was easier for Rushdie to work into his chosen setting. The domestic condition of British Muslims, ignored by the media but hitherto cham-pioned by Rushdie, was such as to make the easy option the dangerous one.

The way forward, made more difficult by recent events, is to seek to assure British Muslims that they are valued. This is not primarily to allow foul-mouthed attacks on their religion to be laughed off, although that might be one side-benefit. Putting Rushdie's book in a more positive light, it is to enable a community to have the self-confidence to speak back rather than shout, and to answer Rushdie's important charges about some aspects of Islam. I, for one, want to know what young Muslim women really feel about their position. Rushdie is right to ask such questions. We must contribute to the conditions under which we might learn the answers. What does not advance matters is to lump all British Muslims together as cohorts of the Ayatollahs and to condemn their cowardice in failing to distance themselves from Iranian warlords. As the Belgian mullah's death demonstrated, Muslims sym-pathetic to tolerance of Rushdie are more likely to be assassinated than is Rushdie himself.

What should be done? Let me offer a, so to speak, novel suggestion. Rushdie could move to Northern Ireland, at least temporarily. This has two immediate advantages. First, the marginal cost of protecting him would be minimal since there is already an enormous security industry and expertise. Second, nobody can get in or out of the island of Ireland without being observed by the authorities so that Iranian death squads would be easily identified and repelled. There are longer-term benefits. It is time that Rushdie stopped trading on his own Anglo-Indian heritage and started exploring other cultural clashes and other forms of fundamentalism. Northern Ireland deserves a good novel from a writer of his calibre. Moreover, if Rushdie were to carry on regardless,

continuing to produce work which challenges other groups, the grievance
of Muslims might be lessened. This is not to recommend a stream of
insults launched against the people of Northern Ireland. Retribution
would be swift. It is to say that the novelist must learn and apply the
lessons of *The Satanic Verses* rather than allow himself, whatever the
provocation, to be stymied by the reaction to it.

Sinn Fein

Having offered Rushdie a home, what might he find here? I imagine that
Rushdie would have some interesting points to make about both Sinn
Fein and the government's propensity to make itself look idiotic in
attempting to cope with the supporters of terrorism. Although the
division between the military and political wings of the IRA is in many
ways cosmetic, it is a sign of hope. The government ought to be
encouraging moves towards constitutional, rather than violent, action.
Censorship of the political wing reflects the opposing viewpoint that
since Sinn Fein commands only minimal support in the island of Ireland,
north and south, it is never going to be satisfied with electoral politics.
Admittedly the self-delusions of the IRA are of major proportions but
once again the solution is not to pretend that the myths are not powerful.
It is to counter fraudulent speech with frank speech. And, for the last
time, it is to state that the underlying problems need to be tackled. If
economic justice between the two communities can be achieved, for
example, millennial claims about uniting Ireland through force would
lose much of their attraction, the IRA would lose much of its passive
support. Restricting Sinn Fein, and then watching the media, who usually
ignore the problems of Northern Ireland, gather to protect the right to free
speech is a diversion from the goal of achieving peace and justice in this land.

Free speech in context

Let me conclude by observing that there are many ways of challenging
intolerance and oppression. Salman Rushdie has tried ridicule and abuse
in *The Satanic Verses*. I prefer Martin Luther King's approach, as
exemplified not only by his campaign for civil rights but also by the
majesty of his language, as for example in his Nobel Peace Prize acceptance speech:

I have the audacity to believe that peoples everywhere can have three meals a day for their bodies, education and culture for their minds, and dignity, equality and freedom for their spirits. I believe that what self-centred men have torn down other-centred can build up. I still believe that one day mankind will bow down before the altars of God and be crowned triumphant over war and bloodshed, and nonviolent redemptive goodwill will proclaim the rule of the land. And the lion and the lamb shall lie down together and every man shall sit under his own vine and fig tree and none shall be afraid. I still believe that we shall overcome.

If we are to overcome obstacles to free speech, it will be in the context of that march towards a society which recognizes our equal dignity. I do not believe that free speech is obtainable in a society unless 'none shall be afraid'. For all the traumas chronicled in the earlier parts of this book, the recent changes in Eastern Europe are a sign of hope that Martin Luther King's prophecy can come true. Free speech has a major part to play in that process and will be a major beneficiary of it. I have the audacity to believe, as I said in the preface, that clear thinking about free speech can also make a contribution. For all the threats to free speech which now beset us, I still believe that we shall overcome.

Notes and Acknowledgements

Chapter 1

The 'Voltaire' quotation can in fact be traced to Evelyn Beatrice Hall, who wrote under the pseudonym of S. G. Tallentyre a book entitled *The Friends of Voltaire* (1906). Her line was intended to capture Voltaire's general attitude. An entertaining book by Paul Boller and John George, *They Never Said It* (Oxford University Press, 1989), relates this story on pp. 124–6.

Chapter 2

The first occasion on which I heard the phrase 'privatization of censorship' was the seminar jointly organized by the Commission for Racial Equality and Interfaith in September 1989; see now their report of that seminar, published as a discussion paper by the Commission for Racial Equality under the title *Law, Blasphemy and the Multi-Faith Society*. On John Philpot Curran, see W. H. Curran's *The Life and Times of John Philpot Curran* (London, 1819).

Chapter 3

In addition to the *New York Review of Books* article quoted in the text, see *Václav Havel or Living in Truth* (Faber, 1987).

Chapter 4

By the time this book is published, the Calcutt Report on Privacy will have been published by HMSO and should be a good guide. At the time of writing the text, the best available account is Raymond Wacks, *Personal Information* (Oxford University Press, 1989).

Chapter 5

The Williams Committee's Report on Obscenity and Film Censorship (*HMSO*, 1979, Cmnd 7772) is the best account of standard liberal arguments. In the USA Report, the Attorney General's Commission on Pornography (1986), presents what it regards as compelling evidence for the harmful effects of pornography. For a robust critique of the male liberal orthodoxy, see Andrea Dworkin, *Pornography: Men Possessing Women* (1981). Perhaps the best writing in this area, from any perspective, can be found in the American professor Catherine MacKinnon's *Feminism Unmodified: Discourses on Life and Law* (1987).

Chapter 6

There is an outstanding article on incitement to racial hatred by Professor Mari Matsuda, from which I have drawn examples; see her 'Public Response to Racist Speech: Considering the Victim's Story' (1989), 87 *Michigan Law Review* 2320.

Chapter 7

The fascinating judgments of the US Supreme Court in the case of Texas v. Johnson are now reported in 109 S. CE. 2533 (1989).

Chapter 8

See Geoffrey Robertson's new edition of *Freedom, the Individual and the Law* (Penguin, 1989), a leading text originally written by the late Professor Harry Street, pp. 262–5.

Chapter 9

Bernard Williams' contribution to the collection by Michael Lockwood, *Moral Dilemmas in Modern Medicine* (Oxford University Press, 1985), is especially valuable on slippery slope arguments. See 'Which Slopes are Slippery?'

Chapters 10–11

Eric Barendt's brilliant synthesis of British, American and Continental legal thinking, *Freedom of Speech* (Oxford University Press, 1985), has been my starting-point on freedom of speech. Even though I often differ from him in my conclusions, I am indebted to him in many ways and especially for his analysis of what is 'speech' and what justifies protecting it.

Chapters 12–16

The afore-mentioned symposium held under the auspices of the Commission for Racial Equality and Interfaith helped shape my thinking on the Rushdie affair. The report includes some source material (e.g. extracts from the English Law Commission Report and the New South Wales law) of relevance to my text. The book I mention, *The Rushdie File*, by Lisa Appignanesi and Sara Maitland (Fourth Estate, 1989) is invaluable for collating press reports and enabling other observers to dispense with their own newspaper cuttings. Those who wish to check dates and comments on the Rushdie affair should therefore turn to this excellent work. Without it, I would have to give a long list of references. For those who do not pursue the matter, however, I should mention that such a list would have revealed the excellent work of many journalists and editors around the world in chronicling events. Just because my text suggests that the pundit columns have, if anything, added to the problems, I do not undervalue the bravery and public service of the news reporting which has, in difficult circumstances, been outstanding. Similarly, the pamphlet produced by the International Committee for the Defence of Salman Rushdie, while obviously one-sided and partial in much of its analysis, is most helpful on the history of blasphemy in English law and I acknowledge my indebtedness to it.

Chapters 17–18

Article 19's report, 'No Comment: Censorship, Secrecy and the Irish Troubles' (1989) is another example of an invaluable source of material, drafted by Ciarán Ó'Maoláin and published extraordinarily quickly. Again, although I think Article 19's interpretation of events is not always definitive, its presentation of information and context is most helpful. I am also happy to acknowledge my debt to Rex Cathcart's history of the BBC in Northern Ireland, *The Most Contrary Region* (Blackstaff Press, 1984). My approach to judicial decisions is explained in my book *Judging Judges* (Faber, 1989).

Chapters 19–21

Joseph Raz's *The Morality of Freedom* (Oxford University Press, paperback edition 1988) has obviously been influential in developing my thinking, although the author (my former tutor) should not be taken to agree with my interpretation of his book, nor with any of my conclusions. To see how my views and arguments on this topic relate to my analysis of other issues of public debate, see my *Law and Morals* (Oxford University Press, 1986).

Index

abortion, 15, 22
Adams, Gerry, 113
  see also Sinn Fein
advertising, 15, 22, 61, 120
Advertising Standards Authority, 16
America, 37, 40, 42, 43, 59
  flag-burning in, 44–7
  Founding Fathers, vii, 19, 24
  judges in, 45–6
  and *Spycatcher* affair, 48–52
  see also Supreme Court, American
Anglicans, as privileged group, 127
  see also Church of England
Anti-Discrimination (Racial Vilification)
    Amendment Act (1989), 90
Archer, Jeffrey, libel case, 24, 32, 33
art, and freedom of expression, 100
Asians, 97
  see also Muslims
Atkins, Humphrey, 109
authors
  freedom of, 95, 96, 98
  provocative, 99, 103, 131

BBC, 13, 16–17, 21
  coverage of Northern Ireland, 109, 113,
    117
Benn, Tony, 23, 100
Birt, John, 13
Bishop of London's Working Party Report,
    82–3, 88
blasphemy, vii, 25, 73, 127
  Anglican reaction to, 82–3, 127
  law of, 74–7, 137
Blom-Cooper, Louis, 16
Bolton, Roger, 109
book-burning
  criticized by Rushdie, 98, 99
  and freedom of expression, 5, 35, 77, 88,
    96
  reported in press, 94
Brennan, Justice, 137

Brighton Bombing, 59
British Campaign against Pornography, 37
British Council for Mosques, 96
Brittan, Leon, 110
broadcasting
  bans in, 111–14, 115
  and judicial decisions, 117, 119
  role of editors and management in, 13, 23
  see also BBC; television
Broadcasting Act (1981), 117
broadcasting authorities, and Northern
    Ireland question, 114
Broadcasting Bill (1990), 23
Broadcasting Standards Council (BSC), 11,
    16–17
Buddhists, 84–5, 88, 103
Bush, George, 23

Campaign against Pornography and
    Censorship, 39
Canada, legislative structure in, 118
Catholics, 84, 126
  in Northern Ireland, 103, 127
censorship, vii, 5, 47, 56, 110, 126, 135
  in advertising, 61
  in Czechoslovakia, 20
  and Northern Ireland, 112–13
  and individual responsibility, 10, 130,
    133
  and mass media, 11–17
Checkland, Michael, 13
Christianity, 73–80, 84
Church of England, 127
  and blasphemy, 82–3
citizenship, 89
civil rights, 113, 119–20, 131, 139
Commission for Racial Equality, 97
copyright, 26, 56, 98
Court of Appeal, 115, 116, 117, 118
Curran, John Philpot, 10, 11, 130, 133

Daily Star, 15

Death on the Rock documentary, 110
Decent Interval (Snepp), 49–50
De l' Esprit (Helvetius), 3
democracy, 23, 60, 65, 80–1
    and law, 116, 119
    and violence, 120–1
Donaldson, Lord, 110–11

Eastern Europe, changes in, vii, 20, 129,
    140
editors and censorship, 15, 98
education, 38, 47, 66, 126, 130
ethics *see* morality
ethnic minorities
    literacy in, 126
    protected, 87
    respect for, 30, 39, 41, 60, 105
European Convention on Human Rights,
    25, 48, 62, 79, 83, 116, 117–18
European Court of Human Rights, 48, 99,
    116
European Court of Justice, 79, 118
expression, freedom of
    as free speech, 61–2, 133
    versus free speech, 35, 44, 57, 60, 105
    and protest, 4–5, 19, 25, 29, 95
    and religious tolerance, 83

Falk, Bernard, 109
fatwa, 4, 73, 76, 89, 97, 100, 101, 131, 133
    see also Khomeini, Ayatollah
feminism, 36, 37, 38
    see also women
Finucane, Pat, viii, 24
flags
    abuse of, and burning, 4, 44–7, 57, 59,
        136
    respect for, 30, 34, 57, 59, 60, 105
Foot, Michael, 98, 100
freedom of expression, *see* expression,
    freedom of
Freedom of Information Acts, 51
free speech
    absolutist interpretation of, 14, 25, 55,
        74, 137
    and advances in media, 21–4
    arguments to support, 55–8
    clarification of terms concerning, 59–62
    concept of, 25, 26, 105, 126
        qualified, 29–30, 130

    and content of speech, 4, 5, 6, 9
    education as pivot of, 38, 47, 66, 126,
        130
    and erosion of liberty, 24, 44–7
    new approach to, 3–4, 139–40
    restrictions to, 48, 50, 90, 112–14, 119
    and rights, 5–8, 25, 133–4
    and values, 40, 43, 51–2, 125, 130, 133,
        136, 140
    willingness to die for, 5, 8, 9, 11
fundamentalism, 95, 97, 103, 128, 130, 138

Gay News controversy, 78–9, 80, 83, 92,
    101
Gibraltar, IRA shooting, 110
glasnost, vii, 129
government, 10, 18, 20–1
    censorship from, 11, 17, 20–1
    and culture, 66, 67
    influence upon media, 17, 23, 61,
        109–11, 119, 131, 139
    and religious toleration, 85–6, 92
    in Rushdie affair, 81
    and *Spycatcher* controversy, 48, 136–7
Guardian, 80, 103

Hale, Chief Justice, 77
Hall, Evelyn Beatrice, 3
Havel, Václav, 20, 100
heresy, 40, 119, 126–7
Holocaust, the, 40, 64
homosexuals, 31, 39, 99
    see also Gay News controversy
hostages and Rushdie saga, 98
Howe, Sir Geoffrey, 6
human rights *see* Universal Declaration of
    Human Rights
Hurd, Douglas, 113

ideas, freedom of, 120, 125–6
identity, 89, 97, 127, 128
impartiality, 117
incitement to hatred, 39–43, 89, 135–6
Incitement to Hatred Act, amendment to
    (1989), 39
Independent, 22, 97, 98
Independent on Sunday, Rushdie's article
    in, 97–101
Independent Television Commission, 24

information technology, effect on free
    speech, 23
International Covenant on Civil and
    Political Rights, 29–30, 39, 76
International Convention on the
    Elimination of All Forms of Racial
    Discrimination, 39–40
IRA, viii, 5, 59, 101, 109–14, 131, 139
irony, misinterpretation of, 55
Islam, Rushdie's critique of, 99
Islamic Society for Religious Tolerance, 94

Jane's Defence Weekly, 50
Jews, 4, 128
    see also Holocaust
Johnson, Gregory Lee, burns American flag,
    44, 45, 46
journalists, 13, 30, 32, 111, 114, 115, 117,
    118, 119, 126, 131, 133
judges, 17, 30, 113
    American, 45–6
    and interpretation of free speech, 59
    in judicial decisions, 116, 117, 118
    liberal, 79
    in Spycatcher controversy, 48–52
justice, 126, 139

Kennedy, Justice, 45
Khomeini, Ayatollah
    death threats of, 4, 73, 76, 89, 97, 100,
        101, 131, 133
    in Rushdie affair, 4, 14, 16, 20, 73
    and threats to free speech, 63, 76, 89, 93,
        97, 131, 137
Kilroy Silk, Robert, 22
Koran, 73
    and group libel, 90
Ku Klux Klan, 7, 42

Lady Chatterley's Lover (Lawrence), 36
language and free speech, 103–4, 120
law, the, 10, 19, 42, 105, 126
    and blasphemy, 74–7, 137
    and breach of confidence, 31
    confusion revealed in, 88–93
    and Northern Ireland legislation, 115,
        116
    and privacy, 134
    promoting toleration, 129–31
    structure of judicial decisions, 116–18

Law Commission, 81, 82, 83, 88
Law Lords, 48–52, 115, 116–17, 118
Levin, Bernard, 15, 80
libel, 25, 30, 32, 34, 56
    group, 89, 90–1, 93
    and newspapers, 22, 24, 33
    and publishing, 14
liberalism, 10, 63, 126–7
    and utilitarianism, 64
liberty, 10, 11
    American belief in, 45
    erosion of, and free speech, 24, 62, 105
    and governments, 66
    and protest, 4–5, 25, 29, 95, 96
Licence and Agreement Act (1981), 117
literacy, and free speech, 126
Llosa, Mario Vargas, 100
Lodge, David, 104
Lords, House of, 116, 119
Luther King, Martin, viii, 139–40

McCarthy, Joseph, 40
McGrory, Paddy, 132
martyrdom, 5
Mason, Lord, 113–14
Maudling, Reginald, 109
Maxwell, Robert, 11, 12, 32
media, mass, 11, 64, 125
    and biased reporting, 44, 133
    and government power, 11, 119–20, 136
    and judicial decisions, 117
    and public scandals, 51–2
    sources of censorship in, 11, 12–19,
        21–4, 110
    see also broadcasting; publishing;
        television
Meese Report (1986), 35–6
Mill, John Stuart, 10, 63, 88
minority groups, 90–1, 96–7, 128
    protected by censorship, 135
    and self-definition, 127, 128
    see also ethnic minorities
Mirror group, 12
morality
    arguments in, 64–8
    and rights, 6–7, 65, 129–30, 133
    and toleration, 130
    and values, 38, 65–7
Morality of Freedom (Raz), 65–7
Morison, Samuel, 50

Most Contrary Region (Cathcart), 111
Mountbatten, Lord Louis, 109
Murdoch, Rupert, 11, 12, 14, 64
Muslims, 24, 84, 87, 89, 90, 91, 92, 94, 128
    offended, 96–7, 99, 101, 105, 125, 126,
    137–8

National Front, 7, 44
nationalism, 44, 46
National Union of Journalists, 15
Nazi party, 5, 41, 44, 64, 94, 137
Neave, Airey, 109
Neil, Andrew, 32
Northern Ireland, 5, 18, 24, 46, 50, 51, 81,
    85–6, 132, 138–9
    legislation on religious toleration, 86, 87,
    103, 127
    nationalists, 103, 104
    television coverage of, 109–14, 119, 133
Northern Ireland (Emergency Provisions)
    Act (1978), 114

Observer, 12, 14
O'Cassey, Sean, 4
offence, 103, 120, 135
official secrets, 48–52, 136–7
Official Secrets Act (1989), 50
orthodoxy, 119
Orwell, George, 8, 11
Owen, David, 113

Panorama, 109
Parekh, Bikhu, 97
Pasternak, Boris, 34
Paul VI, Pope, 126
Pentagon Papers, 49
Pinter, Harold, 98
Places of Worship Registration Act (1855),
    84
pornography, 15, 33, 34, 35–8, 56, 59, 60,
    134
press, 8, 12–13, 14–15, 48, 51, 137
    biased reporting in, 94
    and breach of confidence, 30–1
    changes in, and free speech, 22
    freedom of, 17, 24, 51, 134
    and libel, 32–3, 34
    role in *Spycatcher* controversy, 48
Press Council, the, 11, 16, 17
pressure groups, 22, 37, 113

Prevention of Incitement to Hatred Act
    (1970), 86
Prevention of Terrorism (Temporary
    Provisions) Act (1984), 115
privacy
    and free speech, 134
    intrusion of, 16, 26, 29–34
    respect for, 7, 18, 30, 34, 130
privatization and individual censorship,
    125, 130
propaganda, 39, 40, 113
proportionality, concept of, and
    understanding of free speech, 116, 117,
    118, 119
protest, 4–5, 25, 29, 95, 96
Public Order Act (1986), 87
publishing
    censorship in, 13–14
    exerts pressure on other media, 15–16
    outrage in Rushdie affair, 74, 133, 137

Quakers, 103
Question of Ulster, The, 109

Race Relations Act
    1965, 86
    1976, 86
racism, 39–43, 55, 56, 63, 86–7, 90, 97,
    120, 128, 135–6
    and religion, 85–7, 120
Raphael, Adam, 32
Raz, Joseph, 65–7, 129
Reagan, Ronald, 23, 45–6, 100
Real Lives documentary, 17, 18, 110
Rees, Merlyn, 113–14
Rees-Mogg, Lord, 16, 17
Rehnquist, Chief Justice, 44, 45, 46, 57
religion, 100
    and blasphemy, 76, 78–82, 84
    in multi-faith society, 84–5
    and race, 85–7, 90, 92
    and toleration 127, 130
reporting
    biased, 94, 133
    investigative, 134
    and terrorism, 11, 14, 120
Rowland, Tiny, 11
Runcie, Robert, 82
Rushdie, Salman, vii, viii, 3, 4, 6, 8, 13, 24,
    55, 57, 73–5, 76, 77, 88, 103, 125,

126, 130, 131, 132, 133, 137, 138–9
apologizes for *Satanic Verses*, 3, 94–7
article in *Independent on Sunday*,
    97–101
attitudes to Islam, 129, 138
and racism, 87, 89, 90, 91, 92, 127, 136
see also Satanic Verses, The
Rushdie File, The, (Appignanesi and
    Maitland), 13, 16

Saatchi and Saatchi, 22, 120
Salem el-Behir, vii
Satanic Verses, The (Rushdie), 6, 8, 104,
    105, 129, 131, 137–9
    expression of outrage against, 4, 14, 20,
        22, 23, 24, 73–5, 76, 82, 127
    paperback edition of, 8, 100–1, 132
    see also Rushdie, Salman
Scarman, Lord, 79, 92
secularism, 4, 127
self-regulatory bodies, 11, 16
sexual freedom, 39
Shah, Eddie, 14
Sikhs, 84, 87
Sinn Fein, 5, 7, 101–2, 112, 113, 114, 115,
    118–20, 125, 132, 139
Sky television, 12, 21
Snepp, Frank, 49–50
soap operas, 15, 21, 22
South Africa, 114
Spycatcher (Wright), 7, 17, 22, 23, 30, 48,
    49, 50, 117, 136–8
Stalker, John, 51
statutory bodies, 16–17
Sun, 12
Sunday Correspondent, 22
Supreme Court
    American, 24, 41, 44–7, 49, 99, 105, 136
    Canadian, 118

Television, vii, 8, 16–17, 18, 21, 24
    coverage of Northern Ireland, 109–14

and democracy, 23
satellite, 15, 21, 22
and terrorism, 24, 109–14, 119, 120
terrorism, viii, 5, 18, 64, 95, 101, 131, 132,
    139
Thatcher, Margaret, 6, 15, 17, 73
    and Northern Ireland, 110, 131
Thatcherism, 22, 23
theologians, 82–3
Times, The, 12, 14
Today, 22
trade unions and censorship, 14–15
Twenty-Four Hours documentary, 109

Ulster, 104
Ulster Defence Association, 113, 115
Unionists, in Northern Ireland, 103, 104,
    114
Union Jack, 44
Universal Declaration of Human Rights, 29,
    83, 95
utilitarianism, and rights, 6, 25, 63, 64–5,
    88

Viking Penguin, 73–4, 95, 96, 103, 133
Voltaire, François-Marie Arouet, 3–4, 5, 8,
    9, 132

Wall Street Journal, 42
Ward, Keith, 82
Watergate, 51
Whicker, Alan, 109
Whitehouse, Mary, 78, 101
Who Killed Salman Rushdie? (Clark), 99
Windlesham, Lord, 110
women
    and pornography, 134
    respect for, 30, 36–7, 130, 134–5
    see also feminism
Worsthorne, Peregrine, 32
Wright, Peter, 7, 30, 48, 49
    see also Spycatcher